Causal Knowledge Analytics

Causal Knowledge Analytics

A New Methodology for Business and Social Science Scholars

Yuanyuan (April) Song

Assistant Professor of Management Information Systems, Management Department, Marquette University, USA

Richard T. Watson

Research Director at Digital Frontier Partners, Regents Professor and J. Rex Fuqua Distinguished Chair for Internet Strategy Emeritus, University of Georgia, USA

Xia Zhao

Associate Professor of Management Information Systems, Department of Management Information Systems, University of Georgia, USA

Edward Elgar Publishing

Cheltenham, UK · Northampton, MA, USA

The development of this book is supported by the Alfred P. Sloan Foundation and Wipfli.

Published by
Edward Elgar Publishing Limited
The Lypiatts
15 Lansdown Road
Cheltenham
Glos GL50 2JA
UK

Edward Elgar Publishing, Inc.
William Pratt House
9 Dewey Court
Northampton
Massachusetts 01060
USA

Authorised representative in the EU for GPSR queries only: Easy Access System Europe – Mustamäe tee 50, 10621 Tallinn, Estonia, gpsr.requests@easproject.com

A catalogue record for this book
is available from the British Library

Library of Congress Control Number: 2024952817

This book is available electronically in the **Elgar**online
Business subject collection
https://doi.org/10.4337/9781035353156

MIX
Paper | Supporting responsible forestry
FSC® C013604

ISBN 978 1 0353 5314 9 (cased)
ISBN 978 1 0353 5315 6 (eBook)

Printed and bound by CPI Group (UK) Ltd, Croydon, CR0 4YY

Contents

1. The problem of knowledge accumulation

THE BURDEN OF KNOWLEDGE

Scientific advancements in all fields have been, predominantly, built on previous accomplishments (Kuhn, 1962). However, when Isaac Newton was a scientist, it was a lonely discipline. He had few colleagues, and he was and still is a giant. Today, we have millions of scientists,[1] most of whom are not giants, but contributors of small pieces to the giant jigsaw of scientific discovery across myriad fields. We have produced millions of publications (Park et al., 2023) and that number is increasing, with an overall growth rate of 4.10 percent and a doubling time of 17.3 years (Bornmann et al., 2021).

Scientific progress requires building upon many continually expanding foundations, and this massive combinatorial problem of synthesizing ideas across manifold publications needs supporting technology. Standing on the shoulders of giants becomes more demanding as the body of knowledge grows. Knowledge accumulation results in greater early-life investment in education, but the average age at which great scientists and inventors produce their most important work increased by six years over the course of the twentieth century (Jones, 2010). The burden of knowledge-challenging innovation is also reflected by larger R&D teams and a reduced probability of innovators switching fields. This trend suggests a narrowing scope of scholars' expertise (Jones, 2009). As the body of accumulated knowledge expands exponentially, finding relevant research becomes increasingly challenging, inhibiting researchers' productivity (Bloom et al., 2020). The increasing burden of reviewing published knowledge leads scholars to narrow their scope, which limits the development of discovery and invention (Park et al., 2023).

Historically, the challenge of knowledge accumulation has evolved with technological advancements. The problem of accessing knowledge was recognized in the middle of the twentieth century (Garfield, 1955) and resulted in the development of citation indices for the natural and social sciences.[2] These indices provided researchers with a "wisdom of the crowd" perspective (Surowiecki, 2004) on what a field deems the most relevant contributions to a body of knowledge. Google Scholar, as a full-text search engine, is a digital enhancement and merging of natural and social science indices. While it accelerates the discovery of possibly pertinent research, Google Scholar does not encode knowledge, and scholars return to previous-century practices by reading their search results. Recent artificial intelligence (AI) developments, such as large language models (LLMs), can process text but often struggle with accuracy and reliability issues and fall short in analytical capabilities. The failure to digitally encode knowledge inhibits the growth of many fields. Stacking on the shoulders of others is currently a laborious, tedious, manual task at odds with the digital age and the growth of knowledge.

The other essential process of building on the shoulders of giants is knowledge synthesis, defined as the contextualization and integration of research findings of individual research studies within the larger body of knowledge on the topic (Grimshaw, 2010). Knowledge synthesis integrates what is known and helps scholars see the forest beyond a few trees. However, a review of the literature suggests that knowledge synthesis is loosely guided and weakly supported by information systems (IS). To a large extent, it depends on scholars' cognitive thinking and reasoning. However, the bounded rationality of humans limits their ability to solve complicated problems, such as reviewing a large body of literature and synthesizing its knowledge. Humans' cognitive ability is limited by attentional blink (the time it takes to consciously identify and consolidate a visual stimulus in visual short-term memory), visual short-term memory itself (the restricted amount of visual information that can be held in short-term memory), and the psychological refractory period (in which selecting an appropriate response for one stimulus delays the ability to select a response for a second stimulus) (Marois and Ivanoff, 2005). These limitations highlight the need to leverage the power of IS to assist in identifying and synthesizing related research. Scholars need help in navigating the ever-expanding fountain of knowledge. This book commits to developing methods that utilize IS to assist scholars in handling the burden of knowledge.

KNOWLEDGE ENGINEERING

Knowledge engineering is the branch of engineering that analyzes knowledge about some subject and transforms it into a computable form for some purpose (Sowa, 1999). Knowledge engineering involves acquiring knowledge from experts or a community, representing knowledge in an information system, and utilizing knowledge stored in the system (Studer et al., 1998).

In the realm of social sciences, we have communities generating knowledge. What is lacking is a standard way to represent that knowledge in a computable format and ways to apply and develop methods and tools to utilize the stored knowledge. The purpose of knowledge representation is to store knowledge (in the form of literature) in a format that machines can process. A machine's computational capacity can then be leveraged for the analysis and synthesis of that knowledge. Knowledge engineering provides a path for this process.

Building on knowledge engineering, this book proposes causal knowledge analytics (CKA), defined as the development and application of methods for processing graphical representations of causal models to advance theoretical research by scholarly communities (Watson et al., 2024). CKA involves two primary phases: digitization and analysis. Digitization refers to transforming knowledge into computable formats, making it accessible for machine processing. We discuss the necessity and standards of digitization in Chapter 3, where a framework and procedures for capturing and structuring knowledge are detailed.

The analysis phase involves developing and applying computational methods to the digitized knowledge to derive new insights, test hypotheses, and advance theoretical understanding. Chapters 4, 5, and 6 delve into the techniques used in this phase and demonstrate their potential to enhance scholarly productivity.

THE "KNOWLEDGE AS OBJECTS" PERSPECTIVE

There are multiple perspectives on the meaning of knowledge, with tacit and explicit knowledge representing two main divisions (Nonaka and von Krogh, 2009). Tacit knowledge is "rooted in action, experience, and involvement in a specific context," while explicit knowledge is "articulated, codified, and communicated in symbolic form and/or natural language" (Alavi and Leidner, 2001, p. 110). Because knowledge creation is cumulative, there is no impenetrable membrane dividing the tacit and explicit forms. Each can incorporate elements of the other, with the explicit form more amenable to codification. What originates as tacit knowledge can be converted to an explicit formulation through the use of knowledge exchange protocols (Herschel et al., 2001) – the procedures by which a field formalizes the communication of its findings. For instance, critical scientific discoveries often result from converting fleeting insights into fully fledged explanations. Shannon (1948), the developer of information theory, reports that: "The work wasn't linear; ideas came when they came … one night I remember I woke up in the middle of the night and I had an idea and I stayed up all night working on that" (Soni and Goodman, 2017, Ch. 13). Shannon used mathematics as his knowledge exchange protocol to formalize his theory.

Knowledge also means determining how to use a knowledge store and make sense of the results (Watson, 1996). Additionally, when knowledge is defined as a state of comprehension (Polanyi, 1967), querying and processing a knowledge store can influence and modify one's understanding. While "knowledge as an object" (Bolisani et al., 2012) is just one of the complementary views of the knowledge kaleidoscope (Alavi and Leidner, 2001), it provides a foundation for creating tools and principles to enable knowledge engineering, which can support the other manifestations of knowledge.

CAUSAL KNOWLEDGE

As it advances, science gains in precision and explanatory power (Kuhn, 1962), both of which are usually expressed in abstract, generic, and symbolic form to internationalize comprehension and overcome the inherent ambiguity of language.[3] Each field has a set of symbols that its adherents use for exact communication (such as a chemical reaction of methane, $CH_4 + 2O_2 \rightarrow CO_2 + H_2O$). In physics, Newton's three laws of motion are succinctly defined as causal models (for example $F = dp/dt$). These causal models in their various discipline-specific formalizations are the core of knowledge and the foundation of scientific reasoning (Pearl and Mackenzie, 2018). Humans are intuitive teleological theists (Kelemen, 1999, 2004). Recognizing the most appropriate causal model for a given situation is essential to achieving intentions (Krakovsky, 2022). We innately construct teleological explanations: children demonstrate causal reasoning before mastering a language (Barber and Barber, 2005; Kelemen, 1999). We want to see purpose, cause and effect, in our world and seek interventions (such as a vaccine) to desirably change effects. People seek causal explanations for observations (why do projects fail at alarming rates?), implement interventions for desired consequences (for instance reducing project failure), and are curious about alternatives to past events (counterfactual thinking). However, we have not built a digital social science repository of cause–effect relationships. Rather, scholars must manually extract such knowledge by reading publications. This approach ill-befits the digital age.

Although the importance of causality to scientific progress and human knowledge is well-recognized, philosophers and scientists debate what causality is. This chapter does not intend to exhaustively review the history of the development of causality nor summarize all the various perspectives of causality, since such work requires a book or a series of books. Instead, the goal is to recognize primary perspectives of causality (Table 1.1).

Table 1.1 Various perspectives of causality

Perspective	**Definition**	**Key references**
Probability	X causes Y if X raises the probability of Y $P(Y\|X)>P(Y)$.	Pearl, 2009; Suppes, 1973
Econometrics	If a signal X1 "Granger-causes" a signal X2, then past values of X1 should contain information that helps predict X2 and beyond the information contained in past values of X2 alone.	Granger, 1969
Regularity theory	"An object precedent and contiguous to another, and where all the objects resembling the former are plac'd in like relations of priority and contiguity to those objects, that resemble the latter. C is a cause of e if and only if 1) c is spatiotemporally contiguous to e; 2) c precedes e in time 3) all events of type C are followed by an event of type E."	Hume, 2003 [1739], p. 170

Perspective	Definition	Key references
Experiment	X is a cause of Y if, and only if, there is a possible intervention on X that changes Y.	Holland, 1986; Karahanna et al., 2018; Woodward, 2005
Counterfactual	Causal effects are defined based on comparisons of outcomes that would result from exposure to alternative causal states.	Imai et al., 2011; Morgan, 2013; Morgan and Winship, 2015
Path analytic	Causal inference methods that broadly conceive of causality in terms of graphical models of variables and paths (e.g., structural equation modeling and mediation and moderation models).	Duncan, 1966; Goldberger, 1972
Potential outcomes	This approach considers that each treatment state is associated with a potential outcome and assesses causality based on the relationship between the treatment assignment and the difference in potential outcomes.	Angrist and Pischke 2009; Lee and Lemieux 2010
Configurational view	This view of causality relies on the notion of complex causality using the logic of conjunctural, equifinal, and asymmetric relations.	El Sawy et al., 2010; Mahoney et al., 2013; Misangyi et al., 2017; Ragin, 2014

Causality has been considered an elusive concept. "Most of my colleagues even considered causal vocabulary to be dangerous, avoidable, ill-defined, and nonscientific," said Judea Pearl,[4] which motivated him to build some clarity into the dark view (Pearl, 2009). Motivated by similar reasons, *MIS Quarterly*, one of the leading journals in the IS field, published an editorial article to summarize three views of causality that are most relevant to IS, including path analytic, potential outcomes, and configurational (Mithas et al., 2022). The path analytic view of causality refers to causal inference methods that broadly conceive causality in terms of graphical models of variables and paths (Duncan, 1966; Goldberger, 1972), such as structural equation modeling and mediation and moderation models. The potential outcome approach (that is, counterfactual) considers that each treatment state is associated with a potential outcome and assesses causality based on the relationship between treatment assignment and the difference in potential outcomes. Examples of methods based on the potential outcome approach include instrument variable regression and regression discontinuity design (Angrist and Pischke, 2009; Lee and Lemieux, 2010). The configurational view of causality relies on the notion of complex causality using the logic of relations that are conjunctural (configurations of a set of variables and assessing their impact), equifinal (different configurations may lead to the same outcome), and asymmetric (the presence of a condition leading to an outcome does not necessarily mean that its absence will not produce the outcome) (El Sawy et al., 2010; Mahoney et al., 2013; Misangyi et al., 2017; Ragin, 2014). Experiments are another important approach to establishing causality, such as lab experiments, randomized field experiments, and natural experiments (Karahanna et al., 2018). Experiments enable researchers to control and manipulate extraneous factors and develop causal inferences.

The notion of causality encompasses three distinct levels: association, intervention, and counterfactuals (Table 1.2) (Pearl and Mackenzie, 2018). Association involves looking for regularities in observations and answers the general question: what if I see …? For instance, what does a symptom (a headache, for example) tell me about a disease? Awareness of certain symptoms helps in making diagnostic decisions. The key activity related to this level is observing. The second rung of the causality ladder is intervention, which seeks to answer the question: what if I do …? Continuing the headache example, what if I take an aspirin? Would it cure the headache? The action of interest in this rung is intervening. Suppose that taking an aspirin was not the only action taken to stop the headache; then another question arises: was it the aspirin that stopped the headache? This question could not be answered at the second rung of the causation ladder and belongs to the third level, which is about

Table 1.2 The ladder of causation

Level	Name	Activity	Questions
1	Association	Seeing	What if I see …?
2	Intervention	Doing	What if I do …?
3	Counterfactual	Imagining	What if I had done …?

Source: Pearl and Mackenzie, 2018, p. 28.

counterfactuals and answers the question: what if I had done …? If I had not taken an aspirin, would the headache have stopped anyway?

The ladder of causation provides a framework for revisiting various definitions of causality shown in Table 1.1. The probability perspective is associated with the first level of the ladder: seeing X, what is the probability of Y? Would it be lower without X? A similar idea is pursued in econometrics, such as the idea of "Granger-causes" (Granger, 1969), the family of methods in path analytics, and the regularity theory. Despite various approaches, these perspectives are concerned with the notion of association and thus relate to the first level on the ladder. Interventionist theory precisely captures the second level of causation, where an intervention X affects Y. The counterfactual perspective is closely related to the third level of the causation ladder, which compares the outcome Y (the severity of headache) under alternative states of the cause X (when the aspirin istaken or not taken).

Structural causal models (SCM), developed to capture causality explicitly, consist of two sets of variables, U and V, and a set of functions, f, that assign each variable in V a value based on the values of the other variables in the model (Pearl et al., 2016). The variables U are exogenous, meaning that they are external to the model; researchers choose, for whatever reason, not to explain how they are caused. The variables in V are endogenous (internal to the model).

Every SCM is associated with a graphical causal model, which consists of a set of nodes representing the variables in U and V and a set of edges between the nodes representing the functions in f. This book focuses on acyclic graphs (directed acyclic graphs), defining causality from a causal diagram perspective. If, in a graphical model, a variable X is a child of another variable Y, then Y is a direct cause of X; whereas, if X is a descendant of Y, then Y is a potential cause of X (Pearl et al., 2016). Put another way: a variable X is a direct cause of a variable Y if X appears in the function that assigns Y's value. X is a cause of Y if it is a direct cause of Y, or any cause of Y (Pearl et al., 2016). This book builds on Pearl's view of causality, and the causal diagram tool is used to represent and codify causal knowledge.

Causal knowledge is fragmented and, unless these independent chunks are logically connected, their relationships are essentially invisible. For example, unconnected public fragments might report A → B and B → C, but, unless they are linked through B, the relationship that is A → C can remain undiscovered (Swanson, 1986). Fortunately, causal relationships can be represented as an explicit object in graphical form, which, if standardized, can facilitate the connection of related concepts across objects.

SUMMARY

- The volume of academic literature limits scholarly productivity, and supporting technology is needed.
- Knowledge engineering provides a path to utilizing information systems to master the literature efficiently.
- The "knowledge as objects" perspective provides a foundation for creating tools and principles to enable causal knowledge analytics.
- Causal knowledge, as the foundation of scientific reasoning, can be digitized as property graphs.
- The prerequisite for causal knowledge analytics is a high-quality knowledge store.

NOTES

1. *Unesco Science Report 2021*, unesco.org/reports/science/2021/en/statistics
2. See: clarivate.com/webofsciencegroup/solutions/isi-institute-for-scientific-information
3. The English word "set", for example, has 39 meanings in the Oxford English Dictionary.
4. Judea Pearl's website is bayes.cs.ucla.edu/jp_home.html

2. Comparing CKA with AI

THE KNOWLEDGE RECOGNITION PROBLEM

Nobel laureate Sydney Brenner observed, "We are drowning in a sea of data and starving for knowledge" (Nurse, 2021). In the social sciences, to paraphrase Brenner, "We are drowning in a sea of text and starving for knowledge." Moreover, the sea is choppy. Written statements are often ambiguous and subject to interpretation. Recognizing an article's knowledge is a significant problem, and developing ways to mine the vast accumulated knowledge trove efficiently is an important issue (Larsen et al., 2020; Thilakaratne et al., 2019).

Some progress has been made by using AI to support mining knowledge from text using systematic approaches (Wagner et al., 2021), such as computational literature reviewing (Antons et al., 2021), literature-based discovery (Thilakaratne et al., 2019), and ontological learning (Lim et al., 2020). However, the accuracy of computer-based knowledge recognition is currently insufficient to reach the high level required for practical application in areas such as medicine (Strickland, 2019), bioinformatics (Veuthey et al., 2009), and sociology (Nelson, 2019). The medical literature is perhaps the most critical deposit worthy of knowledge mining. After developing a system for harvesting existing general knowledge effectively and efficiently enough to win a quiz game, IBM thought that, by spinning it off as Watson Health, it had found the means of mining medical knowledge in publications. However, IBM's NLP (natural language processing) technology floundered when trying to make sense of the medical literature. A professor of computer science and AI expert noted, "We're doing incredibly better with NLP than we were five years ago, yet we're still incredibly worse than humans" (Strickland, 2019, 29). AI is currently no match for a medical specialist's ability to interpret medical literature: it has not learned to read like a human expert (Strickland, 2019). Thus, after eight years and billions of dollars of R&D, IBM sold part of Watson Health in early 2022 as it switched its strategic focus (Davis et al., 2022). Further, after seven years of daily text mining to populate a protein sequence database, the Swiss Institute of Bioinformatics concluded that, "many of these information retrieval and extraction tasks could be greatly simplified with the requirement of metadata at the article submission time" (Veuthey et al., 2009). There is no reason to assume that social science knowledge is more tractable (Nelson, 2019), because text mining cannot resolve equivocality (Al Fawareh et al., 2008; Stokoe et al., 2003), and cannot detect true from false (Denning, 2023).

In the social science domain, rule-based systems, such as CauseMiner (Mueller and Huettemann, 2018), and ML (machine learning) approaches, such as DeepCause (Mueller and Abdullaev, 2019), report accuracies of about 80 percent for extracting cause-effect relationships. Such a level of accuracy helps improve the identification of appropriate literature but is not sufficient, we assert, for analytics. Data precision is critical for getting value from analytics. The existing evidence is that machines currently do not match human capabilities for knowledge recognition and subsequent codification. Hence, we propose a method that relies on humans to provide the wherewithal for extracting knowledge before conducting high-quality analytics. In this respect, we differ from those who are developing software to recognize, extract, and codify knowledge. Software can be beneficial for analyzing codified knowledge, but we contend that the initial codification is best done by humans. To support the ultimate goal of causal knowledge analytics, we need a high-quality knowledge store, which is achieved through rigorous human-based processes. Humans can interpret nuances, resolve ambiguities, and apply contextual understanding that current AI systems cannot replicate. By leveraging human expertise in knowledge extraction and codification, we can create a robust foundation for subsequent computational analysis.

LITERATURE REVIEW TOOLS

Various tools support literature reviewing (Table 2.1). Extracting knowledge using machine learning is one focus in the current literature, including DeepCause (Mueller and Abdullaev, 2019) and TheoryOn (Li et al., 2020). These tools utilize machine learning to identify and extract causal relationships.

Another stream of research focuses on developing tools to help scholars find related articles efficiently. For example, full-text search engines (such as Google Scholar) enable keyword searches. ASReview uses

Table 2.1 AI-based tools

Purpose	Method/tool	Description	References
Knowledge extraction by machine learning	TheoryOn DeepCause diskNET	Extracting causal knowledge using deep learning and NLP	Chen et al., 2020; Chen et al., 2021; Dann et al., 2019; Li et al., 2020; Mueller and Abdullaev, 2019
Relevant research identification and content extraction	Google Scholar Web of Science ResearchRabbit Semantic Scholar LitSonar Dimensions OpenAlex Scopus Crossref openAIRE Litbaskets ASReview	Full-text search engines with various filtering and screening features	scholar.google.com webofscience.com researchrabbit.ai semanticscholar.org litsonar.com (Sturm and Sunyaev, 2019) dimensions.ai openalex.org scopus.com crossref.org openaire.eu litbaskets.io (Boell and Wang, 2019) asreview.nl (van de Schoot et al., 2021)
Relevant research identification and content extraction	Automated detection of implicit theory (ADIT) technique	Identifies relevant research using machine learning	Larsen et al., 2019

Purpose	Method/tool	Description	References
Relevant research identification and content extraction	Open knowledge maps	Grouping publications based on text similarity Helping identify relevant concepts	openknowledgemaps.org
Relevant research identification and content extraction	VOSviewer	Visualizes bibliometric networks	vosviewer.com
Relevant research identification and content extraction	Iris.AI	Description-based search, various filters, machine-generated summaries	iris.ai
Relevant research identification and content extraction	SciSpace	Description-based search, machine-generated summaries, able to answer questions about a paper	typeset.io
Relevant research identification and content extraction	SourceData	Extracts biological objects from figures, which makes relationships hidden in figures searchable	sourcedata.embo.org
Relevant research identification and content extraction	Elicit	Finds relevant papers based on questions	elicit.org

Purpose	Method/tool	Description	References
Relevant research identification and content extraction	Scite	Identifies relevant research by enriched citation information (e.g., where, when, and how one paper is cited by another)	scite.ai
Tools designed to address jingle and jangle fallacies	Inter-Nomological Network	Predicts whether two constructs with different names refer to the same phenomenon	Larsen and Bong, 2016; Li et al., 2020
Theory integration framework	Theory representation meta-model	Proposes a meta-model that represents causal theories and a taxonomy of inter-theory relationships	Mueller, 2015
Empirical synthesis	MetaBUS	Semi-automated extraction of empirical findings Enables quick search of research findings Assists meta-analysis	metabus.org (Bosco, 2022; Bosco et al., 2020)

machine learning algorithms to predict publication relevance (van de Schoot et al., 2021). Tools are being developed to predict if jingle or jangle fallacies exist in the literature, which helps in accurately distinguishing between different theoretical constructs or identifying when the same construct is referred to by different terms (Larsen and Bong, 2016). MetaBUS is another significant tool that synthesizes empirical findings across studies. By aggregating data from multiple sources, MetaBUS provides an overview of research trends and empirical evidence, facilitating meta-analyses and helping researchers draw more robust conclusions.

While these tools represent an improveement in managing the growing volume of academic literature, they fall short in providing direct access to knowledge or offering advanced analytical capabilities. In the next section, we detail how CKA distinguishes itself from AI approaches and addresses these limitations.

THE DISTINCTIVENESS OF CAUSAL KNOWLEDGE ANALYTICS

The key differences between the AI-based approach and CKA (Table 2.2) reveal that CKA are complementary approaches to improving literature reviewing, reporting the nature of existing knowledge, and

Table 2.2 Key differences between causal knowledge analytics and other approaches

Features	**Other approaches:** machine learning (e.g., TheoryOn) and AI (e.g., LLM)	**Causal knowledge analytics**
Source	Unstructured text	Standardized digitized knowledge objects
Computation	No support for computing relationship metrics	Wide variety of methods of relationship metrics
Information processing methods	Neural networks and NLP	Graph query language, social network analysis, information theory, association analysis, correspondence analysis, and extensible to include new methods

Source: Watson et al., 2024.

exploring causal connections. We consider these differences using an input-processing-output (IPO) approach.

Large language models (LLMs) process unstructured digitized text files and PDFs. Text is inherently ambiguous at all levels of linguistic analysis (Piantadosi et al., 2012). The frequency of syntactic and semantic ambiguity is a significant challenge to NLP. Furthermore, current LLMs do not model ambiguity (Liu et al., 2023), and the essential structures and characteristics of language do not seemed to have evolved for precise communication (Chomsky, 2002, p. 107). To apply an old information systems adage, *ambiguity in – ambiguity out.* In contrast, standardized coding and measurement are means for reducing ambiguity. The metric system replaced thousands of local measurement systems, which reduced ambiguity in trading.[1] Databases are designed to reduce ambiguity by defining entities, relationships, and attributes. This makes databases powerful platforms for operational management and analytics, but databases do not eliminate ambiguity. Fields containing text strings, such as a concept's definition, can be ambiguous because they are based on everyday language.

The nature of an input determines how it might be processed. Clearly, the range of processing possibilities is higher with structured data because some fields are suitable for direct computation or counts. Furthermore, text fields in a database can be processed using NLP and LLM methods. A database is designed to support analytics, and thus many information processing options are available. Graph mining methods based on machine learning are facilitated by graph-represented causal knowledge. Link-prediction methods can suggest undiscovered causal relationships (Zhang and Chen, 2018). Community detection methods can cluster concepts and identify research themes (Chen et al., 2017). The fundamental difference is that an LLM "does not compute" and was not designed for mathematical manipulations. CKA is based on well-established metrics and analysis methods, while the performance of LLMs is highly dependent on the input text.[2] Although augmenting the volume of input data for LLMs could improve their performance, this approach is a computationally expensive strategy, which also has significant environmental costs.[3, 4]

Because CKA is based on a graph of concepts and their relationships, it intrinsically supports a synthesizing concept-centric literature review (Webster and Watson, 2002), which is generally accepted as more appropriate than an author-oriented summarization. LLMs can summarize a collection of articles, but the integration of knowledge across many sources may include hallucination or confabulation because LLMs lack reasoning. Synthesis is a higher-level human task than summarization because it involves understanding a phenomenon from diverse perspectives, which CKA can support. Ultimately, humans have to make sense of a set of CKA analytics, LLM outputs, and relevant original texts, including those not having a causal model, to document a comprehensive understanding of a topic. These approaches are complementary methods for discovering what is known in order to investigate the unknown. Measurements are critical to science. "Science cannot progress without reliable and accurate measurement of what it is you are trying to study. The key is measurement, simple as that," as put by Robert Hare.[5] CKA adopts and develops measurements to evaluate the knowledge frontier, which is distinct from LLMs. Scientific advances are built upon cumulative contributions and complementary methods. LLMs have the potential to assist causal knowledge analytics, but their current capabilities are insufficient for synthesizing academic articles (Watson et al., 2024).

SUMMARY

- **Challenges in knowledge extraction**: Accurate knowledge extraction from ambiguous text remains a significant challenge for current AI and NLP technologies. These technologies struggle with the nuances and complexities of human language, necessitating human-led codification to ensure reliability and accuracy in analytics.
- **Limitations of AI-based tools**: While there are numerous AI-based literature review tools available, they fall short in providing direct access to the knowledge embedded in texts and in developing robust measurements and analyses for coded knowledge.
- **The need for standardized digitization and advanced analytics**: There is a critical need for methods that not only digitize knowledge in a standardized format but also enable advanced analytical capabilities. Developing such methods would bridge the gap between data retrieval and knowledge synthesis.

NOTES

1. Prior to the adoption of the metric system, France, for example, had over 250,000 local measurement variants (Zupko, 1990).
2. *The Economist*, August 12, 2023: www.economist.com/business/2023/08/13/ai-is-setting-off-a-great-scramble-for-data

3. IEEE *Spectrum*, September 24, 2021: https://spectrum.ieee.org/deep-learning-computational-cost
4. *Nature*, February 20, 2024: www.nature.com/articles/d41586-024-00478-x
5. Interview with Alix Spiegel, *All Things Considered*, May 27, 2011: www.npr.org/2011/05/27/136723357/creator-of-psychopathy-test-worries-about-its-use

3. Knowledge digitization

THE INEVITABLE DIGITAL TRANSFORMATION

Organizations have increasingly realized the importance and value of data analytics since the development of the relational database model and SQL (structured query language). Analytics facilitated by digitization have profoundly impacted organizations, such as improving customer engagement (Bijmolt et al., 2010), boosting supply chain performance (Trkman et al., 2010), and promoting innovation (Duan et al., 2020). Organizations that ignore digital transformation are unlikely to thrive or even survive.

The history of digital transformation can be traced back to the 1960s and 1970s when computers first began to be used in business settings, automating basic tasks like payroll processing and inventory management. The pivotal point occurred with the advent of personal computers and the development of the relational database model by E. F. Codd. The relational database model, along with the subsequent development of SQL, provided a standardized way to store, retrieve, and manipulate data. This breakthrough laid the foundations for modern data analytics and business intelligence tools. As computing power increased and costs decreased, more organizations began to leverage these technologies to gain insights from their data. The rise of the internet and the availability of big data further accelerated digital transformation. E-commerce pioneers like Amazon and eBay demonstrate the power of leveraging data and analytics to create personalized customer experiences and optimize operations.

Such a profound transformation has not touched academia. While the indispensability of digital transformations to improve productivity and data mining to inform business decision-making are widely acknowledged (e.g., Gurbaxani and Dunkle, 2019; Hagiu and Wright, 2020; Wixom et al., 2013), mining social science knowledge is a green field. If we exclude PDFs, very little of this vast literature has been digitized. As a result, there is a lack of analytical methods to assist scholars in processing knowledge.

The academic field could benefit tremendously from digital transformation. In a similar way to industry practice, with knowledge digitized in a standardized manner, analytics could be utilized to extend scholars' ability to process the literature, improve their productivity, and enable them to reach the knowledge frontier more efficiently. We refer to this approach as causal knowledge analytics: the development and application of methods for processing graphical representations of causal models to advance theoretical research by scholarly communities (Watson et al., 2024).

STANDARDIZED KNOWLEDGE DIGITIZATION

The burden of knowledge growth highlights the need to build information systems to assist in reviewing and synthesizing. The starting point and foundational work are to digitize knowledge. We focus on coding causal inferences and process models and details of their source publication as graphs. Graphs have an inherent nature of simplicity, consisting of only two main objects, nodes and edges. Such conciseness makes graphs easy to standardize. This reduces the level of ambiguity, which is another challenge of the existing approaches of literature reviewing. Currently, the dominant approach to communicating knowledge is through text, but written statements are often ambiguous and subject to interpretation, which often undermines the efficiency and accuracy of knowledge communication in the information systems community and many other academic fields. Furthermore, a common practice of literature reviewing is to employ textual analysis, such as text mining, to facilitate structuring and managing knowledge. However, text mining cannot resolve equivocality or make an ambiguous statement less ambiguous (Al Fawareh et al., 2008; Stokoe et al., 2003). Researchers still struggle with obliqueness when comprehending and interpreting text mining results to support literature reviewing. Equivocality is an intrinsic flaw of communicating through text. It is why an entire profession exists – Law – to argue about the meaning of documents, including their use or misuse of punctuation.[1]

Nodes and edges (i.e., relationships) are key components of a graph, and labels and other properties are used to provide specific information about the nodes and edges and improve the scholarly value of a knowledge database. We define seven types of nodes for representing a causal model as a graph, including Author, Publication, Element (a general term for concepts, constructs, and events), Relation, Definition, Model, and Theory. Edges, represented as arrows, are relationships among nodes (Figure 3.1). Notice that we need to create a node for a relation (the Relation node) to record the type of relationship (such as causal, mediating, or moderating) between two concepts (Song et al., 2024; Watson and Webster, 2020).

Table 3.1 Definitions of features in causal model graphs

Term	Definition
Elements	An element is a general term for a concept, construct, or process. Elements, and Relations connecting them, build a causal or process model.
Concept	A concept is semantically defined by its association or usage with other terms that are not directly observable.
Construct	A construct references constitutive components of a concept, but the component parts are not directly observable.
Variable	A variable is an operational term that specifies the activities or operations necessary to measure it (Van de Ven, 2007).
Event	Events are the natural units of the social process; what kcy actors do or what happens to them (Van de Ven, 2007).

Elements (defined in Table 3.1) can connect to Relation, Model, and Publication nodes. A Model node indicates whether a model is proposed (based on theories), revised (based on empirical results), or has some other origin. A Publication node stores a publication's citation-related information. An Element's definitions are recorded using Definition nodes and relate to corresponding Element nodes and Publication nodes providing the definition. Theories are captured using Theory nodes, which can relate to Publication, Model, and Element nodes depending on how a theory is discussed in an article. Authors of a publication are included in Author nodes and are linked to corresponding Publication nodes. An example of the graph representation of a publication (Ou et al., 2014) is shown in Figure 3.2 and the associated Cypher code is given in Appendix 1.

Labels group nodes into sets, and all nodes that have the same label belong to the same set. For example, we group concepts, constructs, and processes into one set labeled as "Element". Various colors can be used

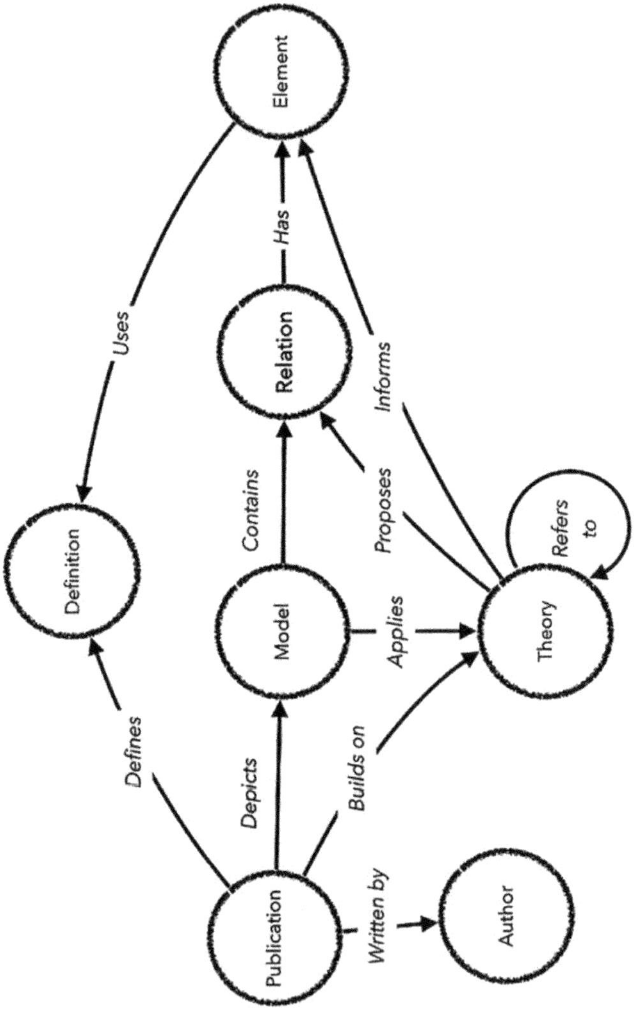

Source: Song et al., 2024.

Figure 3.1 *Overall framework of the causal model analysis approach*

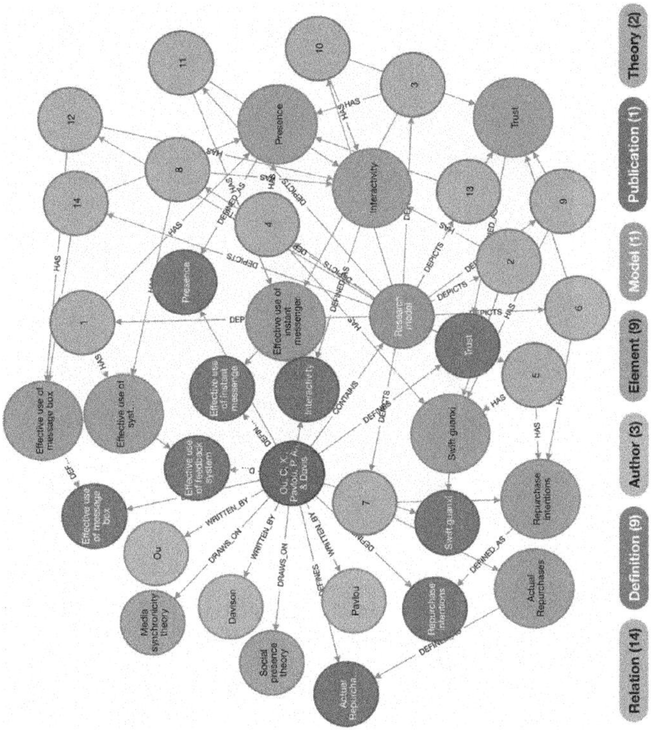

Source: Ou et al., 2014.

Figure 3.2 Graph representation of a publication

to indicate different types of node, such as theories, authors, and definitions (see Figure 3.2). Edges between nodes are labeled according to their relationships. For example, a publication is *written by* authors; a publication *defines* concepts; a publication *contains* a research model.

Properties describe nodes and relationships. For example, "Element type" is a property of an element with the value of a construct, concept, or event (defined in Table 3.1). Concepts are at a higher level of abstraction than constructs. Concepts and constructs are building blocks of grand theories and middle-range theories, respectively (Van de Ven, 2007).

Table 3.2 Definitions and properties of nodes

Node	Definition	Property	Property value	Unique identifier
Publication	Publication that contains causal or process models	DOI ISBN Citation Year	DOI of a publication, if available ISBN of a book, if available Citation information in APA format Publication year	UUID
Element	A general term for a concept, construct, or event	Element name Element type	Name of the element concept, construct, or event	Element name
Definition	Definitions of an element	Definition name Definition	Name of the element that the definition describes Element definition	UUID
Relation	Relationship between elements	Relation number Relation type	Numbering relations in each model starting from 1 Causal, mediating, moderating, correlational, or process	UUID

Node	Definition	Property	Property value	Unique identifier
Model	Model that depicts causal or process relationships	Model name Model type	For example, "research model", "causal", "correlational", "process", or "hybrid"	UUID
Theory	Theory that informs elements, relations, research models, or publications	Theory name	Name of a theory	Theory name
Author	Author of a publication	First name Middle name Last name ORCID	First name of an author Middle name of an author, if applicable Last name of an author ORCID of an author	UUID

To retrieve information precisely, each type of node must have a property that can serve as its **unique identifier**. We adopt several strategies to uniquely identify nodes. We leverage existing unique identifiers as much as possible, such as a digital object identifier (DOI)[2] or international standard book number (ISBN) for a Publication node.[3] When there is no node property that can be used as a unique identifier, we create a universally unique identifier (UUID) (Lal, 2015). A UUID generator creates a 128-bit value that is unique across space and time. Implementing a UUID facilitates the insertion of each publication's coded causal model into a graph database, where each node remains uniquely identified as the database grows. It means that coding can be distributed rather than centrally controlled. Details of properties and unique identifiers are available in Tables 3.2 and 3.3. Detailed coding guidance is given in Appendix 1.

Table 3.3 Relationships and their properties

Relationship	Properties and value
(Publication)-[:Written by]->(Author)	Author order
(Publication)-[:Builds on]->(Theory)	–
(Publication)-[:Depicts]->(Model)	–
(Publication)-[:Defines]->(Definition)	–
(Model)-[:Applies]->(Theory)	–
(Model)-[:Contains]->(Relation)	–
(Relation)-[:Has]->(Element)	Role: 'antecedent', 'consequent', 'mediator', 'moderator', 'control'
(Element)-[:Uses]->(Definition)	–
(Theory)-[:Informs]->(Element)	–
(Theory)-[:Proposes]->(Relation)	–
(Theory)-[:Refers to]->(Theory)	–

Source: Song et al., 2024.

CODASAURUS: AN APPLICATION TO FACILITATE PUBLICATION CODING

Coding publications by a third party is not an efficient long-term solution. Ideally, authors provide the code as part of the review process and add it as an appendix to their publication (Song et al., 2024). We developed an application, Codasaurus, using the Shiny package in R to simplify the process for authors and third-party coders, such as those preparing a literature review.[4] This app can generate Cypher code for a graph version of a publication (Figure 3.3). The flowchart of coding papers with Codasaurus is provided in Appendix 2.

1. Publication

   Scholars input the DOI, ISBN, or publication citation by clicking an option in the drop-down list. We recommend DOI or ISBN when available, as the app generates the citation using an API to access the Crossref database.[5]

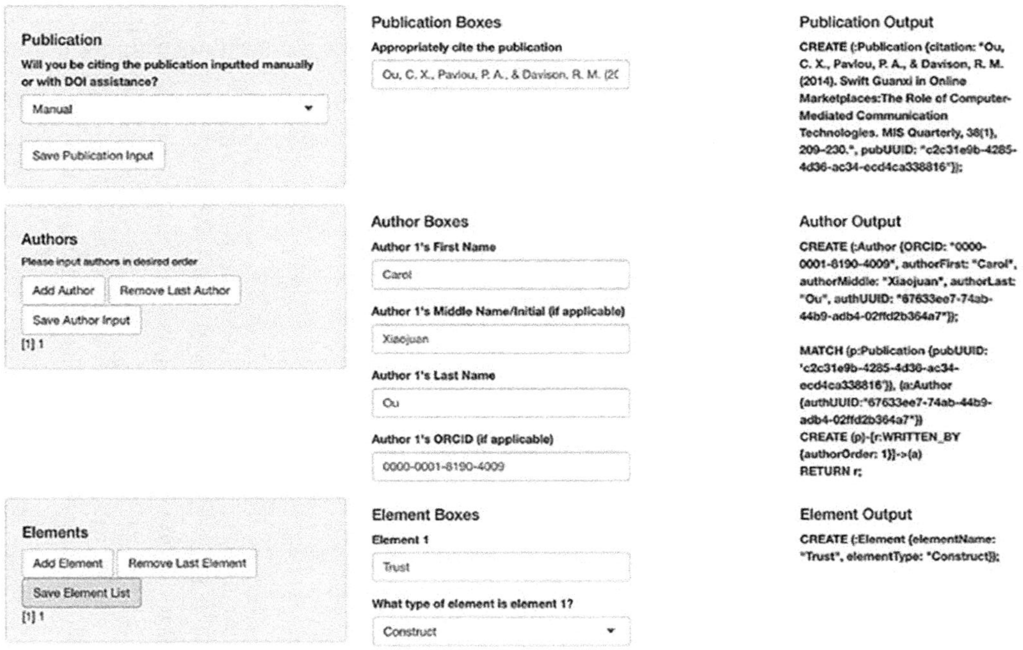

Source: Song et al., 2024.

Figure 3.3 *The Codasaurus application developed to facilitate publication coding*

2. Author

This section requires details of authors, including their ORCIDs (if they have one), first, middle (if applicable), and last names. We recommend authors acquire ORCIDs and use them for academic identification. If the ORCID is provided, the app retrieves an author's details from the ORCID database. When a DOI is provided for a publication, ORCIDs will be automatically entered for each author when they are part of the DOI record.

3. Model

Coders need to name the causal models included in a publication.

4. Element

For each element, three inputs are required: element name, type, and definition. The element type includes construct, concept, or event (defined in Table 3.1). Concepts are at a higher level of abstraction than constructs (Van de Ven, 2007). A variable specifies the method necessary to measure a concept or construct (Van de Ven, 2007). Events are the natural units of the social process (Van de Ven, 2007). Coders should define each element. Coders are shown existing definitions for the element, and they can either choose one or provide a new definition.

5. Relation

For each relationship, the coder enters the relationship type (i.e., causal, mediating, moderating, correlational, or process), chooses the model to which the relationship belongs (for example "research model"), selects elements included in the relationship, and specifies the role of each element (i.e., antecedent, consequent, mediator, or moderator). The description of a relationship is optional.

6. Theory

The coder needs to specify how a theory is used: "a publication builds on a theory", "a theory informs an element", "a theory proposes a relationship", "a theory refers to another theory", or "a model applies a theory".

We have created a sample, publicly available database, enabling scholars to query a set of 238 coded publications.[6] We encourage the IS field to adopt this method, or some extension of it, to code new papers so the field can accumulate details of publications to build a graph database of its core knowledge.

SUMMARY

- **Embracing digital transformation**: Organizations have harnessed digital transformation to enhance productivity, customer engagement, and innovation. Academia needs a similar shift to improve research efficiency and effectiveness.
- **Necessity for standardized knowledge digitization**: The scientific community lacks a standardized approach for digitizing knowledge. A graph-based framework is proposed to systematically organize scholarly knowledge, improving knowledge accessibility and computability.
- **Introduction of the Codasaurus app**: Codasaurus has been developed to support model codification. This interactive tool simplifies the coding process, enabling researchers to code a paper in approximately 15 minutes.

NOTES

1. See, for example, *The New York Times*, 9 February, 2018: www.nytimes.com/2018/02/09/us/oxford-comma-maine.html
2. www.doi.org
3. www.isbn.org
4. https://t-rex-graph.org/codasaurus
5. www.crossref.org
6. https://t-rex-graph.org/analysaurus/

4. Methodology foundations

DEFINING AND QUERYING A GRAPH

Graph description language (GDL) creates graphs by defining the nodes and edges, and their properties in a graph. Graph query language (GQL) is a programming language for interrogating graph databases (for example Neo4j[1]), and visualizing, manipulating, and retrieving nodes and edges. GQL is a declarative language, and it can be used for describing what a computation should perform without specifying how to achieve it (Francis et al., 2018). Graph query languages are similar in their querying power to relational database query languages (such as SQL), and are generally more efficient for writing queries for recursive relationships and relational chains. Creating databases and retrieving relevant data are usually the initial steps of performing an analysis, making this method critical for CKA. Cypher, as both a GDL and GQL, is used to create and query causal model databases. The key Cypher syntax is summarized in Appendix 3.

VIRTUAL GRAPHS

GQL can also be used to create and manipulate virtual graphs, which are not physically stored in a graph database. Virtual graphs can be full or partial copies of existing graphs,[2] or consist of virtual nodes and relationships created for temporary analysis. Virtual graphs offer flexibility in graph manipulation, as the graph database is not changed permanently. The advantages of using virtual graphs include:

- Focused visualization. Coded papers can quickly expand to the extent that visualizing the entire database is not feasible, and coders might need to focus on a portion of a graph. Virtual graphs can extract a subset of the graph database (such as a causal model) for visualization and analysis.

- Non-destructive exploration. Virtual graphs allow for experimental restructuring and analysis without altering the original database, preserving data integrity.
- Restructuring for visualization. Analysts can remodel the graphs and present a more intuitive visualization of causal models. Coding relationships as Relation nodes ensures the fidelity of the database, but it makes the visualization of a model less intuitive. The following code extracts the causal model in a coded paper (shown in Figure 3.1), and the resulting virtual graph is presented in Figure 4.1.

```
MATCH (c:Element)<-[:HAS{role:"consequent"}]-
(r:Relation{type:"causal"})-[:HAS{role:"antecedent"}]->(a:Element),(r:Relati
on{type:"causal"})<-[:DEPICTS]-(m:Model)
WHERE toLower(m.modelTitle)="research model"
WITH DISTINCT a, c
RETURN a,c,apoc.create.vRelationship(a,"RELATES_TO",{type:"causal",
model:"Research model"},c)
```

The transformation results of various relation types are listed in Figure 4.2. In causal relationships, the transformation is straightforward. The original structure, where A causes B, is maintained in the DAG representation. Mediating relationships, where A affects B through mediator M, are also readily represented in DAG. The transformation preserves the causal chain, showing how the effect of A on B is transmitted through M. Moderating effects are not specified in DAG (discussed in detail later), as it is non-parametric, and effect modification is not considered in DAG analysis. Instead, each variable is understood as a moderator in DAG (Pearl, 2017). To align our method better with DAG analysis, we label the relationship between antecedent (A) and moderator (M) as *Interacts with* and the relationship between moderator (M) and consequent (B) as *Relates to*, which is consistent with other element relationships. When scholars run DAG analysis (for example backdoor path), a virtual graph without *Interacts with* relationships can be created.

NATURAL LANGUAGE PROCESSING

Natural language processing (NLP) uses algorithms to understand and process human language. The methods in this book apply NLP by using text similarity analysis and stemming.

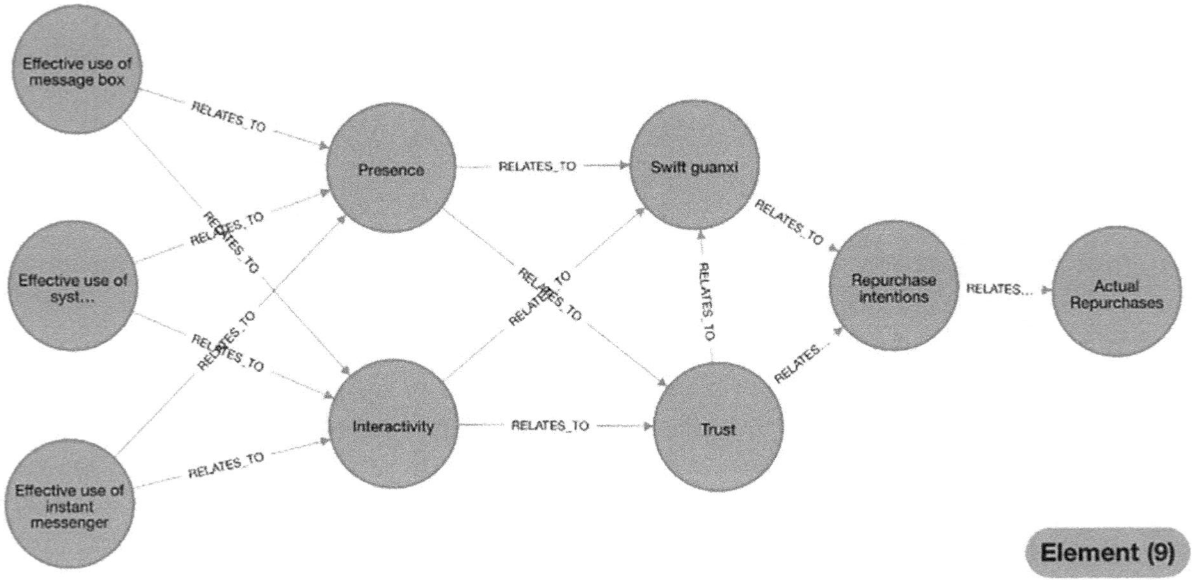

Source: Song et al., 2024.

Figure 4.1 *Virtual graph that extracts and presents a causal model*

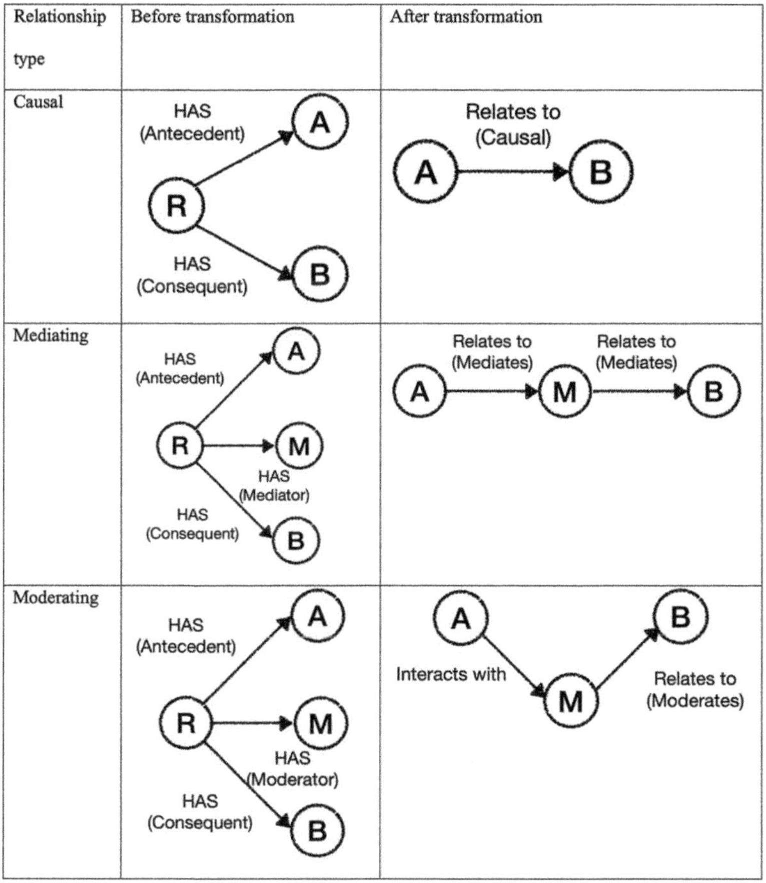

Source: Song et al., 2024.

Figure 4.2 Model transformation for various relation types

Text similarity analysis

Semantic similarity can be measured using various techniques, such as string-based, corpus-based, or knowledge-based similarity, and bidirectional encoder representations from transformers (BERT) (Devlin et al., 2018; Gomaa and Fahmy, 2013).[3] String-based similarity measures operate on string sequences and character composition (Gomaa and Fahmy, 2013). Jaccard similarity, for example, calculates the percentage of overlap between sets of words (Jaccard, 1912). Corpus-based similarity determines word similarity based on a corpus (Islam and Inkpen, 2008). A popular corpus-based algorithm is latent semantic analysis (Landauer and Dumais, 1997). Knowledge-based similarity algorithms identify the degree of similarity between words by matching the meanings of words based on semantic networks (Mihalcea et al., 2006), for example WordNet,[4] which is a well-accepted source of matching word semantic meanings (Budanitsky and Hirst, 2006; Mihalcea et al., 2006; Miller, 1995). Python and R provide packages to support similarity analysis based on WordNet.[5]

BERT (Devlin et al., 2018) builds a bidirectional architecture that allows a model to learn the context of a word from those both preceding and following it in a sentence. The training of a BERT model has two steps: pre-training and fine-tuning. The pre-training corpus is from the BooksCorpus (800 million words) and English Wikipedia (2,500 million words), and it is publicly available.[6] The pre-trained model can be fine-tuned to adapt various NLP tasks, such as text similarity. For the method in this book, a pre-trained model is applied.

Stemming

Stemming is an NLP technique to simplify words by removing their suffixes. Reducing words to their root forms allows analyses to accommodate labeling variance, such as "behavior intention" and "behavioral intention". Word stemming allows unifying variants of concept and theory names. This book implements the widely adopted Porter algorithm (Willett, 2006). Concept and theory names are processed to find their root words, which are stored in the property of "stem". Entered queries are stemmed and matched with the root words of concept and theory names.

CONCEPTUAL ISOMORPHISM

Identifying similar graphs (graph matching) is an important element in graph theory (Conte et al., 2004). Its application in social sciences is to identify similar causal models. For a labeled graph, similarity is determined by two factors: structural and semantic (Song et al., 2021). A weighted average of structural and semantic similarity is defined as conceptual isomorphism (Song et al., 2021), which is calculated in two steps: 1) calculating the structural similarity between two models using graph matching methods (Caetano et al., 2009; Yan et al., 2016); and 2) computing the semantic similarity between concepts using NLP. The workflow of this method for a jungle conundrum[7] is summarized in Figure 4.3.

Structural similarity is measured by graph edit distance; that is, the least number of editing operations (such as adding or deleting vertices or edges) needed to transform one graph into another (Gao et al., 2010). When two graphs have the same structure, the graph edit distance is zero, and they are isomorphic (McKay and Piperno, 2014). Graph edit distance is an error-tolerant measure of graph structural similarity, which computes the number of edit operations necessary to make two graphs isomorphic (Gao et al., 2010).

In Figures 4.4 and 4.5, several edit operations are necessary to make the two graphs isomorphic: deleting node e and its connections with

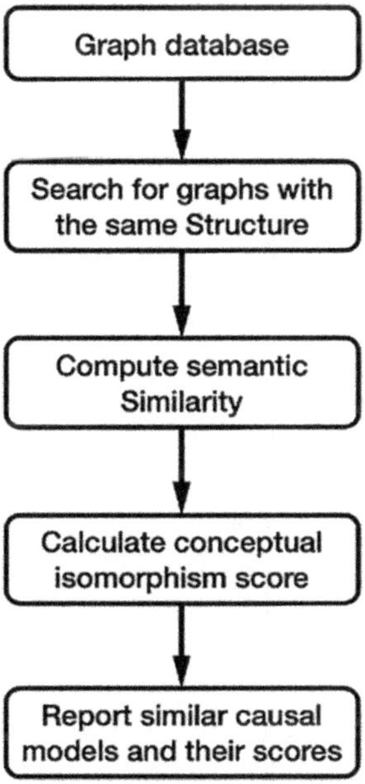

Source: Song et al., 2021.

Figure 4.3 *A solution for a jungle conundrum*

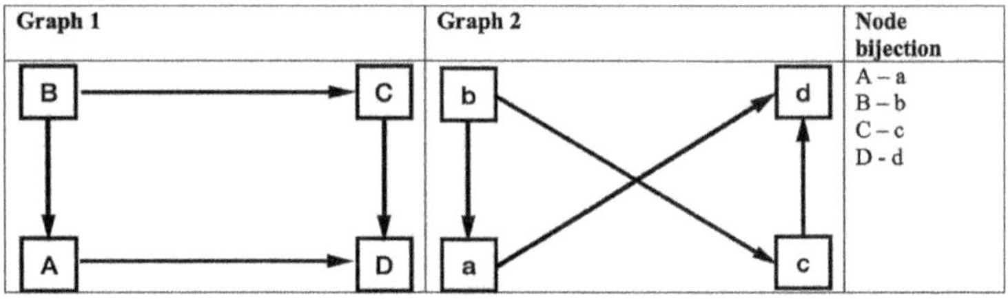

Source: Song et al., 2021.

Figure 4.4 Graph isomorphism

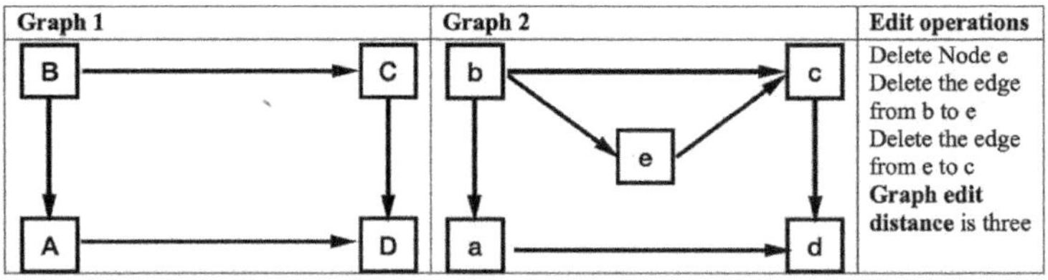

Source: Song et al., 2021.

Figure 4.5 Graph edit distance

other nodes. Although, by deleting node e, all associated edges are automatically deleted, the graph edit distance is three, not one, because it is a count of changes of nodes and edges rather than steps. After making such changes, there exists a bijection preserving node adjacency (A–a; B–b; C–c; D–d). A smaller number of edit operations indicates a higher similarity between the two graphs.

Semantic similarity refers to the likeness between the labels of corresponding nodes (that is, concept name similarity) based on isomorphic bijection (for example the semantic similarity between A and a, and B and b). Concept similarity is determined by computing the similarity between corresponding concepts using WordNet.[8]

The computational complexity of graph edit distance grows exponentially as the size of the graphs (the number of nodes) increases (Zeng et al., 2009). Two types of algorithm are developed to calculate graph similarity: (1) accurate algorithms, which emphasize precision but can be slow with large graphs, and (2) speedy algorithms, which opt for estimation to enhance speed (Abu-Aisheh et al., 2015). In our method, we apply an accurate algorithm with a time limit for each pair of graphs (10 minutes, for example), and, if the computation exceeds the time limit, the estimation algorithm is used to generate an approximation.

NETWORK ANALYSIS

A network can represent real-world problems, such as social networks for relationships among social entities, transportation networks for mapping transport infrastructure, and scholarly networks depicting citation metrics among publications. Network analysis provides a set of measures to study the structure of a network and identify nodes and edges that play an important role in the network (Table 4.1).

Table 4.1 *Network science measures*

Measure	Definition
Closeness centrality	Calculates which nodes have the shortest paths to all other nodes (Freeman, 1978)
Betweenness centrality	The number of these shortest paths that pass through a node (Freeman, 1977)
In-degree centrality	The number of outgoing edges a node has in a network (Freeman, 1978)
Out-degree centrality	The number of incoming edges a node has in a network (Freeman, 1978)
Eccentricity	The length of the longest shortest path with any other node
Diameter	The longest eccentricity in a graph
Periphery index	$\frac{\text{Eccentricity}}{\textit{Diameter}} \in (0,1]$
Cut-points	A critical node whose removal causes disconnection
Constraint	The extent to which a node's access to potential structural holes is constrained by its current contacts (Burt, 1992)
Effective size	The number of non-redundant contacts of a node (Burt, 1992)
Efficiency	The ratio between effect size and the number of contacts
Concept density	The ratio of the number of concepts shared among models to the total number of concepts

Betweenness centrality represents the degree to which nodes are linked with each other. A node with high betweenness centrality has a stronger influence over the flow of "information" in a graph.

Closeness centrality measures how close a node is to all the other nodes in the network. A node with the highest closeness centrality has the shortest distances to all other nodes. Therefore, in social networks, closeness centrality is a way of detecting nodes that can spread information efficiently through a network.

Degree centrality counts the number of immediate contacts that a node has in a network. In a directed graph, degree centrality can be classified into two types: out-degree and in-degree centrality, based on the direction of the edge. In social networks, degree centrality is used as an indicator of popularity (Verweij, 2012). In causal model networks, nodes with high out-degree centrality are fundamental antecedents. Nodes with high in-degree centrality are popular consequents.

Similar to learning nodes having central roles, it is helpful to identify nodes that are on the edge of a graph. Eccentricity and diameter determine whether a node is close to the **periphery** of a graph. The eccentricity of a node is the length of its longest shortest path to all its connected nodes (Wasserman and Faust, 1994). The maximum eccentricity of all nodes is the diameter of the graph (Wasserman and Faust, 1994). The ratio of a node's eccentricity to a graph's diameter (the periphery index) is the extent to which a node is close to the edge of a graph. A node with a periphery index equal to one is on the edge of a graph. When the periphery index is zero, indicating that eccentricity equals zero, a node is isolated and has no connection with the rest of the network.

$$periphery\ index = \frac{\text{Eccentricity}}{Diameter} \in [0,1]$$

Cut-points are critical nodes in a network, whose removal causes disconnection. They unite a causal model network and ensure its essential connectivity. This analysis is helpful in identifying theories, concepts, and publications that amalgamate the knowledge of a field.

Structural hole measures, defined as the separation between non-redundant contacts, originated in a social network context (Burt, 1992). Structural holes are indicators of opportunities where individuals can reach non-redundant contacts and the associated network benefits. The existence of a structural hole between two people indicates that their contacts are, to some extent, additive and not redundant, and thus can provide non-redundant network benefits. In causal model networks, structural holes are missing links between non-redundant concepts.

Redundancy occurs if two contacts are connected or structurally equivalent, referring to the extent to which people are connected with the same group. To illustrate, B and C in Figure 4.6 are redundant to A as a result of a direct relationship between B and C. In Figure 4.7, B and C are redundant to A because B and C are both connected with D and E.

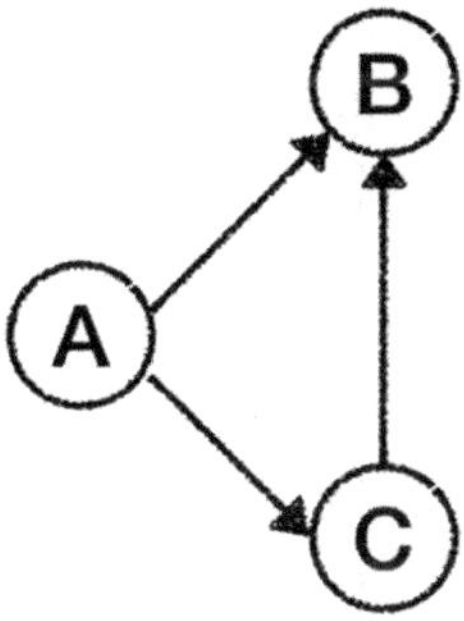

Figure 4.6 *Redundancy by a direct relationship*

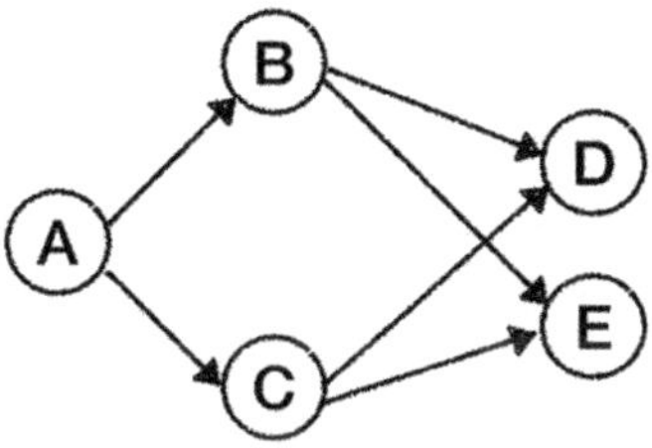

Figure 4.7 *Redundancy by structural equivalence*

Several measures are developed to identify structural holes, including **effective size**, **efficiency**, and **constraint**. Effect size measures the number of non-redundant contacts of a node, calculated by the size of a node's contacts minus the redundancy among the contacts. A higher effect size means a node has more non-redundant network benefits. Efficiency is the ratio between effect size and the number of contacts. A constraint is an indicator of structural holes, which measures the extent to which a node's neighbors are connected. A high constraint indicates a person's contacts are more connected, and there is less "empty space" between contacts in a person's network. This limits a person's access to structural holes.

The idea of structural hole theory is closely related to weak tie theory. The strength of a tie, in the social network context, is defined as a combination of time, emotional intensity, intimacy, and reciprocal services that characterize the tie (Granovetter, 1973). The key argument in weak tie theory is that, the stronger the tie between A and B, the more overlap they have in their friendship circles, and that the information flow in a network largely depends on weak ties (just acquaintances). Weak ties allow one to reach information and social entities that strong ties (family and friends) cannot offer and to integrate otherwise disconnected contacts (Granovetter, 1973).

Density is a common measure of network structure. In a social network context, information can flow more easily and efficiently in a network with higher density. In the causal model context, **concept density** measures how connected a network is by computing the ratio of the number of concepts shared among models and the total number of concepts. Concept density indicates the level of knowledge fragmentation. A low number of shared concepts indicates that most concepts appear only in one paper and therefore have a high level of knowledge fragmentation.

DAG THEORY

Scholars often deal with more than one causal relationship in a study, and causal diagrams are useful to depict and capture multiple relationships among variables. Causal diagrams use graph notation (nodes and edges), where nodes represent variables and arrows represent a causal effect between two variables. A keystone of research on causal diagrams is directed acyclic graphs (DAG); that is, graphs with no directed cycles (Pearl, 1995). DAG is a powerful tool to visualize and explicate the assumptions underlying a model and decide whether the assumptions are sufficient for obtaining consistent and unbiased estimates of outcome variables (Pearl, 1995).

DAG theory provides a framework and a set of criteria to help researchers evaluate causal models. Graph presentation serves as a visual aid to facilitate and simplify the analysis of potential biases. DAG theory also provides potential ways to adjust biases. Conducting DAG analyses is beneficial during research design and data collection processes by addressing potential biases at an early stage. DAG can also be used to scan the coded models in a domain to identify formulation issues. D-separation, confounding, a backdoor path, and selection biases are common bias-identifying criteria.

D-separation (d denotes directional) is a set of rules to determine the dependence or independence between variables (Geiger et al., 1990). Two variables are d-separated if all paths between them are blocked. Two variables are independent if they are d-separated. The following is the set of rules to decide if a path is blocked or open.

D-separation rule 1: If there are no variables conditioned on, a path is blocked when two arrowheads collide at some variable on the path (Figure 4.8).

Model	**D-separation**
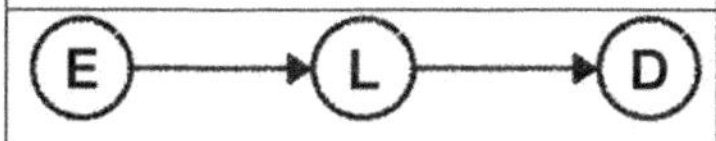	The path between E to D is open
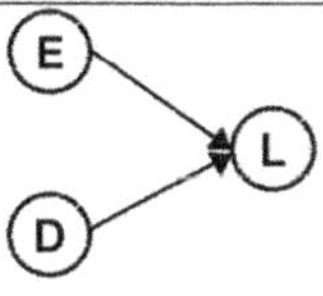	The path between E to D is blocked by collider L

Figure 4.8 *D-separation rule 1*

D-separation rule 2: Any path that contains a non-collider that has been conditioned on is blocked. For instance, in Figure 4.9, the path between E and D is blocked if conditioning on L, which is a non-collider.

Figure 4.9 *D-separation rule 2*

D-separation rule 3: A collider that is conditioned does not block a path. The path between E and D in Figure 4.10 is open if conditioning on L.

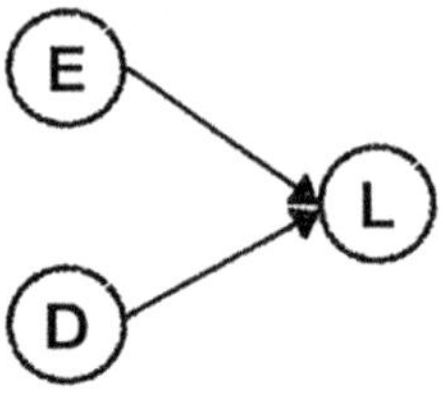

Figure 4.10 D-separation rule 3

D-separation rule 4: A collider that has a descendant that has been conditioned on does not block a path. In Figure 4.11, the path between E and D is open if conditioning on S.

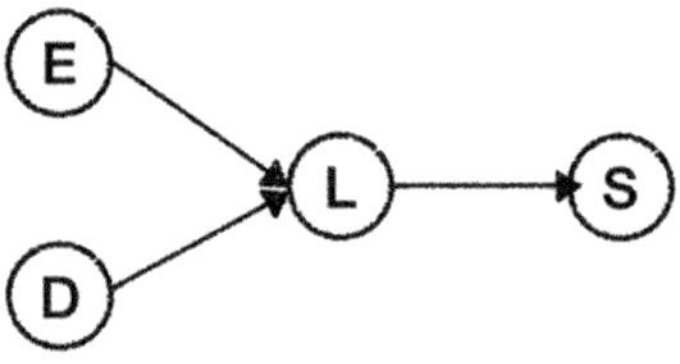

Figure 4.11 D-separation rule 4

Confounding occurs when there is a common cause of the independent and dependent variables. A DAG illustration of confounding is shown in Figure 4.12, where L is the common cause of E and D. Confounding is problematic because it is difficult to make a causal conclusion between E and D without controlling the effect of L. DAG theory uses the backdoor path criterion to address this problem.

A **backdoor** path of E to D, defined as a path that connects E to D and has an arrowhead pointing to E, is a common cause between E and D. Backdoor path criterion is used to decide if the causal effect of interest

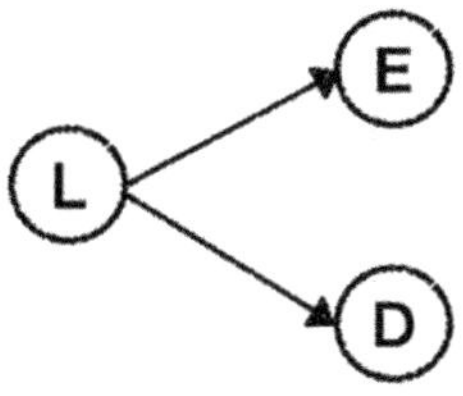

Figure 4.12 *DAG illustration of confounding*

is identifiable and what adjustment is required to identify the effect. The effect of E on D is identifiable if either: there are no backdoor paths from E to D, or measured covariates are sufficient to block all backdoor paths from E to D. For instance, L is the backdoor path between E and D inFigure 4.12, and the effect of E on D is identifiable only after conditioning on L, which blocks the backdoor path between E and D. Another example of a backdoor path is E-L-S-D in Figure 4.13. Conditional on S, L, or both of them will block the backdoor path between E and D.

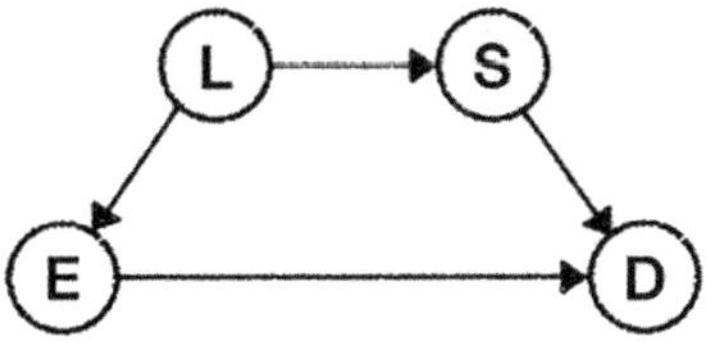

Figure 4.13 *Example of a backdoor path*

Selection bias occurs when research subjects differ systematically from the population of interest, which can lead to inaccurate conclusions. While selection bias can result from various causes (such as volunteer bias, non-respondence bias, and so on; Sackett, 1979), the causal inference underlying selection bias is the same (Hernan et al., 2004). Let E, D, and L denote genetic factors, environmental factors, and cancer respectively (Figure 4.9). If L is being conditioned on (that is, all research subjects have cancer), it is very likely that the cause of cancer is genetic for a subject who does not experience any environmental factors. In other words, among people with cancers, the likelihood of genetic causes is higher for those not influenced by environmental factors. That is because, in the absense of environmental factors, the occurrence of L still needs to be explained. Therefore, conditioning on L causes E and D to be associated, even though they might be independent. The principles of DAG theory can be applied to causal knowledge networks to identify potential confounders and possible approaches to address confounders. For instance, R packages, such as ggdag and dagitty,[9] are suitable.

ASSOCIATION RULE ANALYSIS

Association rule analysis was developed to identify items that frequently appear in the same transactions (Agrawal et al., 1993). Business analytics have utilized it to improve decision-making, such as product placement and marketing strategy (Halim et al., 2019). Apriori is one of the most commonly used algorithms for association rule analysis.[10] Association rules are usually represented in the form of "antecedent → consequent". Both the antecedent and the consequent can be one item or a set of items. The rule implies that if the antecedent appears in a transaction, the consequent is likely to occur with a certain level of confidence and support (Table 4.2). In the context of causal models, items are concepts and transactions are models. When applied to causal models, association rule analysis can identify concepts that tend to appear in the same causal models. GQL can query a database and return the relationship frequency between the antecedent and the consequent.

Table 4.2 Association rule measures

Term	Definition
Support	The proportion of the times a concept set, including both antecedent and consequent, occurs in the database
Confidence	The probability that a rule is correct, which is a ratio of the number of models containing both antecedent and consequent to the number of models containing antecedents
Frequency	The counts of directional relationships from antecedent to consequent in a graph database

CORRESPONDENCE ANALYSIS

Correspondence analysis, which visually displays a contingency table in a multidimensional space (Greenacre, 1984), is a useful approach for exploring relationships between concepts and variables in information systems (Watson and Brancheau, 1991; Watson et al., 2015). Correspondence analysis can visualize the rows (for example curations) and columns (for example concepts) in a contingency table. Each point represents a row (curation) or a column (dependent variable). If two rows (or columns) are similar in terms of their relationships with columns (or rows), they are closer on the map (Greenacre, 1984). The distance between two points indicates their similarity (Hoffman and Franke, 1986; Yelland, 2010). Visualizations created by correspondence analysis reveal the relationships between and within two variables. One application of correspondence analysis is examining the association between concepts (such as frequent dependent concepts) and research topics.

INFORMATION ENTROPY-BASED MEASURES

Information entropy measures the uncertainty or randomness of a system (Shannon, 1948). Entropy is highest when the level of uncertainty is greatest, such as when all events have an equal probability of occurrence. In contrast, entropy is lowest when there is little variation, such as when the probability of occurrence is dominated by a single event. Similar to the information compression index developed by Watson et al. (2022), we define a causal consensus index (CCI), where X, Y, and D represent antecedent, consequent, and dependent concepts, respectively, as:

$$s = -\sum_{i=1}^{n} f_i * log_2 f_i \text{ where } f_i \text{ is the relative frequency of } X_i,\ Y_i, \text{ or } D_i$$

$$max_n = -log_2 \frac{1}{n}$$

where n is the total number of X, Y, or D

$$CCI = \left| \frac{s}{max_n} - 1 \right|$$

The lowest CCI (where CCI = 0) indicates no consensus, and a higher CCI means a higher level of consensus, with CCI = 1 indicating complete consensus. The calculation and interpretation of CCI for each consensus type are summarized in Table 4.3. Dependent consensus is computed in the same manner as antecedent consensus.

Table 4.3 *Causal consensus types*

Consensus type	Definition	Diagram illustration
Antecedent consensus	The level of agreement in terms of what antecedents (X+) precedes a concept (Y)	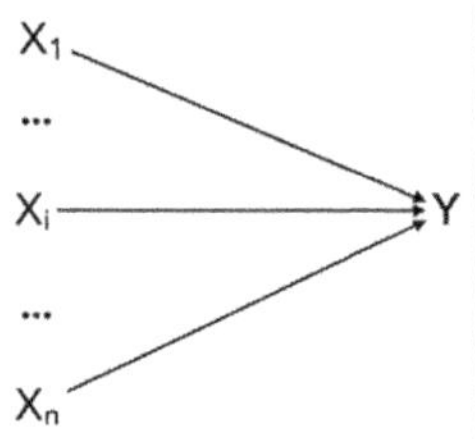
Consequent consensus	The level of agreement in terms of what consequents (Y+) follow a concept (X)	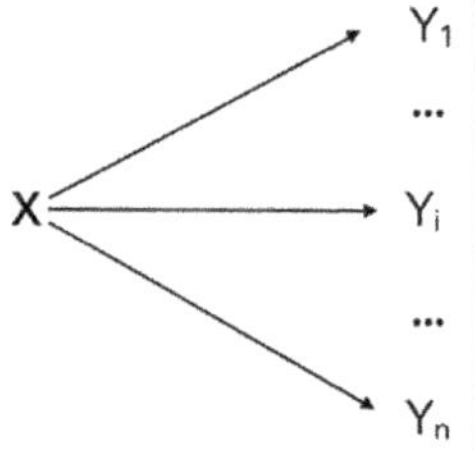

UPSET

UpSet is a visualization technique (Lex et al., 2014) for presenting rich set-intersecting information. Figure 4.14 and Table 4.4 show an example of UpSet and its corresponding data.

In Figure 4.14, each row of the matrix represents an information system, and each column represents a vulnerability condition. The visual representation features solid dots (●) to denote vulnerabilities (columns) impacting each information system (a row). For example, Microsoft is associated with three vulnerabilities, indicated by the three dots in the top horizontal bar. Vertical bars represent the size of a vulnerability collection. The second column indicates that Microsoft and Citrix share common vulnerabilities. The horizontal bars reveal that Microsoft and Citrix are related to five vulnerabilities and one vulnerability, respectively. In

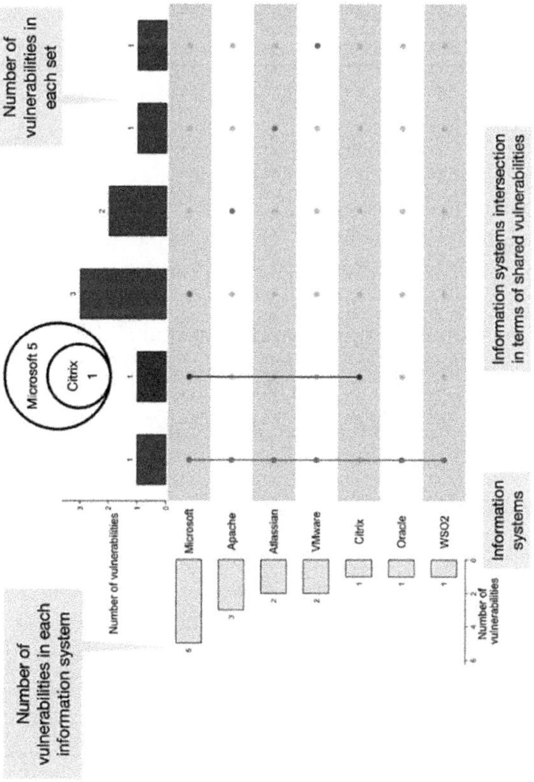

Figure 4.14 Example UpSet presentation

Table 4.4 Illustrative data for an UpSet visualization

Vendor	Product	Vulnerability condition
Microsoft	Exchange server	Remote code execution
Microsoft	Exchange server	Security feature bypass
Microsoft	Exchange server	Elevation of privilege
Atlassian	Confluence server and data center	Arbitrary code execution
Apache	Log4j2	Remote code execution

the case of Microsoft, five is the sum of the values above the three left-most vertical bars.

The strength of an UpSet visualization is its information richness, including information on sets (such as information systems), set attributes (such as vulnerabilities), and set intersecting (information systems sharing vulnerabilities). Because of this strength, UpSet has been adopted in many disciplines, including biology (e.g., Hentze et al., 2018), psychiatry (e.g., Visser et al., 2020), and astronomy (Lyu et al., 2022). UpSet also appears in prestigious journals, such as *Scientific Reports* (Boesl et al., 2024), *Nature Medicine* (Corridoni et al., 2020; Hentze et al., 2018), and *Science* (Winding et al., 2023).

SUMMARY

- **Defining and querying a graph**: Graph description language and graph query language (such as Cypher) create, visualize, and query graph databases. GQL can also create virtual graphs for temporary visualization and analysis subsets without altering the database.
- **Natural language processing**: NLP is used to process text fields in publications, specifically through stemming and text similarity analysis.
- **Conceptual isomorphism**: Conceptual isomorphism identifies similar causal models based on structural similarity measured by graph edit distance, and semantic similarity measured using WordNet.
- **Network analysis**: Network analysis measures network structure to identify important nodes and edges. Key measures include centrality (betweenness, closeness, in-degree, out-degree), diameter,

eccentricity, periphery index, cut-points, constraint, effective size, efficiency, and concept density.

- **Directed acyclic graphs**: DAG theory helps to evaluate causal models and identify biases such as confounding, selection bias, and backdoor paths.
- **Association rule analysis**: Association rule analysis finds relationships between variables in large datasets, identifying patterns and correlations.
- **Correspondence analysis**: Correspondence analysis is a multivariate statistical technique that visualizes contingency tables, identifying relationships between variables.
- **Information entropy**: Information entropy measures the uncertainty or randomness in data, assessing the level of consensus in knowledge networks.
- **UpSet**: This is a technique for rich set-intersecting visualization.

NOTES

1. https://neo4j.com
2. https://neo4j.com/labs/apoc/4.1/virtual/virtual-graph
3. Other methods, such as large language models (LLMs), could be used.
4. https://wordnet.princeton.edu
5. www.nltk.org/howto/wordnet.html and https://cran.r-project.org/web/packages/wordnet/index.html
6. https://github.com/google-research/bert
7. A jungle conundrum is the problem of identifying similar causal models from a vast knowledge network (Song et al., 2021).
8. See https://wordnet.princeton.edu. Other transformers and language models could be used to calculate concept similarity.
9. https://cran.r-project.org/web/packages/dagitty and https://cran.r-project.org/web/packages/ggdag
10. See https://cran.r-project.org/web/packages/arules/index.html for an implementation.

5. Analysis framework for causal knowledge analytics

This chapter proposes a five-level analysis framework for causal knowledge analytics (Figure 5.1 and Table 5.1). Concepts and constructs are the building blocks of grand theories and middle-range theories, respectively (Van de Ven, 2007). Concepts are at a higher level of abstraction than constructs. A concept is semantically defined by its association or usage with other terms that are not directly observable. A construct references constitutive components of a concept, where the component parts are not directly observable. A variable specifies the method necessary to measure a concept or construct (Van de Ven, 2007). Events are the natural units of the social process; they are what key actors do or what happens to them (Van de Ven, 2007). Concepts and constructs are not isolated; they are connected through causal (and process) relationships, which are

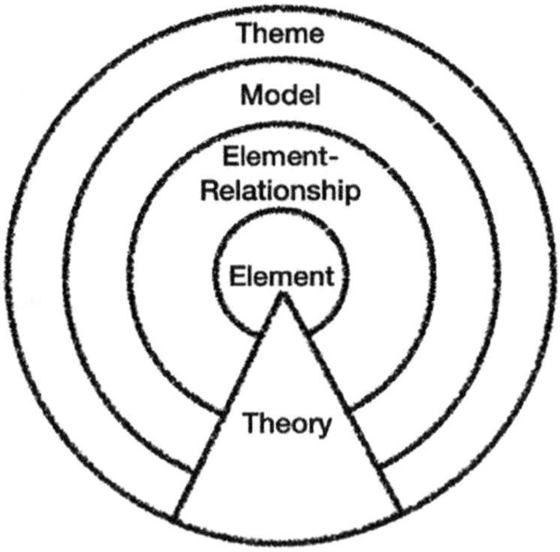

Figure 5.1 Five-level analysis framework

the core of social science knowledge. Several relationships around the same topic build a research model, and a set of research models studying the same phenomenon form a research theme. Theories, as the foundation of the field of information systems (IS), are associated with the above four levels. A theory can inform a concept, explain a causal relationship, build a research model, and relate to a theme of literature.

Table 5.1 Five levels of analysis

Level of analysis	Example task	Method
Element	Querying publications, definitions, theories, research models, and topics related to a concept	Graph query language (GQL)
Element	Analysis of concept semantic similarities	Natural language processing (NLP)
Element–Relationship	Retrieving antecedents, consequents, frequency of antecedent or consequent pairs, and causal chains of a concept	GQL
Element–Relationship	Querying mediators and moderators	GQL
Element–Relationship	Interpreting concepts' network position	Network science metrics
Model	Identifying similar causal models	Graph isomorphism; NLP
Model	Identifying concepts that tend to appear together in a model and reporting relationship frequency	Association rule analysis
Theme	Evaluating the density of a knowledge network	Network science metrics
Theme	Concept-curation correspondence analysis	GQL; correspondence analysis
Theme	Identifying potential brokers in a concept-relationship network	Structural hole theory

Level of analysis	Example task	Method
Theme	Assessing knowledge development; specifically, how concepts' effective size changes over time	Structural hole theory
Theme	Assessing causal consensus	Information entropy
Theory	Finding theories and their frequency in a knowledge network	GQL
Theory	Analysis of the impact of a theory in a knowledge network	GQL; correspondence analysis

Source: Watson et al., 2024.

For each level, we identify a set of analyses and the supporting methods. We demonstrate the utility of the proposed analysis by analyzing a set of MISQ (*MIS Quarterly*) Curations papers. The results are presented in Chapter 6. The five-level analysis is facilitated by a web-based application, Analysaurus.[1]

ELEMENT LEVEL

The element-level analysis focuses on concepts, constructs, and events. Because concepts are fundamental building blocks of theory development, a concept-level analysis covers how concepts are defined in the literature, similarities among these definitions, what publications examine a concept, what theories inform a concept, and what topics are associated with a concept. GQL (graph query language) queries can search for publications, definitions, topics, and theories associated with a concept.

It is common that a concept has multiple definitions. For example, one review reports 23 different definitions of "digital transformation" (Vial, 2019). The jingle and jangle fallacies – in which two concepts have identical (different) labels but reference different (same) real-world phenomena – highlight the importance of being conscious of definitions beyond concepts' names (Kelley, 1927; Thorndike, 1904). Understanding how concept definitions vary and change is fundamental to understanding a domain (Goertz and Press, 2006). Natural language processing (NLP) can process concept names and definitions and compute their pair-wise similarity. A bidirectional encoder representations from transformers (BERT) technique (Devlin et al., 2018) can determine semantic similarity.[2]

ELEMENT–RELATIONSHIP LEVEL

Elements without their networks of relationships in a conceptual model are an incomplete description of knowledge. Identifying relationships associated with a concept requires scholars to read and synthesize across publications. In contrast, a graph database connects fragmented relationships in individual publications, and knowledge graph analyses can quantify the assessment and surface concepts with critical roles in a network, including concepts on a network's periphery, concepts with central roles, and concepts that bridge causal models. Eccentricity and diameter determine whether a node is close to the periphery of a graph. Concepts on the edge of a causal model network are tangential to the field, or innovative, and have not been explored extensively. Measures of in-degree, out-degree, and betweenness centrality inform the central roles of concepts. Association rule mining, originally developed to discover co-occurrences of items within a transaction (Agrawal et al., 1993), can be applied to analyze which concepts tend to appear in the same model, suggesting symbiotic relationships. Understanding the role a concept holds in a network is challenging without appropriate metrics. These analyses contribute to the defragmentation of knowledge by revealing the full extent of conceptual connections in a corpus.

MODEL LEVEL

The problem of identifying similar causal models from a vast knowledge network is defined as the jungle conundrum (Song et al., 2021). That is, a knowledge network is a massive array of tendrils; however, computers can hack through these to reveal a path forward. The approach to solving the jungle conundrum based on graph theory and NLP is described in Chapter 4. DAG analysis can be applied to codified models and analytical packages to assist in identifying potential issues in establishing causality.

THEORY LEVEL

Theories guide knowledge creation. With a graph representation of a knowledge network, we can identify theories that relate to an element, which would inform researchers of various theoretical perspectives of a concept or phenomenon. A starting point for examining the various theoretical contributions to a domain is to examine the frequency with which various theories inform related topics.

Social network analysis can assess the importance of a theory in a knowledge network. High degree centrality suggests that a theory is frequently referenced in the literature. High closeness centrality could indicate that a theory has a direct influence on other concepts and publications in a knowledge network. High betweenness centrality could suggest that a theory is between many nodes in their linkages with each other and indicates its influence on the network.

THEME LEVEL

Theme-level analysis evaluates the state of knowledge at the topic level. We analyze the level of knowledge fragmentation in curations, how various curations converge, how knowledge develops over time, and the level of agreement at the knowledge frontier. The methods employed to provide useful metrics include network connectivity analysis, correspondence analysis, structural hole measurements, and information entropy determination. Concept density indicates the extent to which concepts are studied in multiple publications – a lower concept density indicates a higher level of knowledge fragmentation. Constraints and effective size are measures of structure holes, indicating potential brokers in a network. The causal consensus index is a measure adapted from information entropy, which states the extent of agreement in the literature.

ANALYSAURUS: AN APPLICATION TO FACILITATE CKA

Analysaurus is a web-based application that has been developed to facilitate causal knowledge analytics. It provides scholars with efficient and direct access to core knowledge in publications. The app offers analysis across five levels: concept, relationship, model, theme, and theory. It connects to a graph database of coded articles, allows users to specify their scope of analysis with a set of filters, and includes the five-level analysis discussed previously (Figure 5.2).

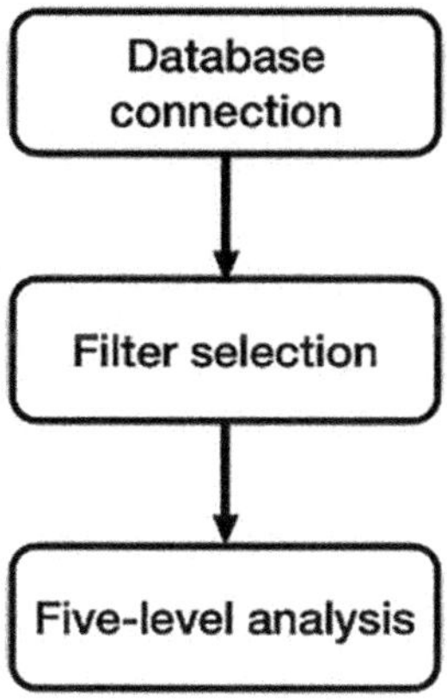

Figure 5.2 *Flowchart of Analysaurus process*

The available database for this app includes a set of publications in the IS field, but scholars can connect it with their personal databases. The available filters include:

- Field. Scholars can select the specific academic disciplines relevant to their research. This filter ensures that the analysis is conducted within the context of the chosen fields, enabling more targeted analysis.
- Period. This filter allows users to define the time frame for their analysis. By selecting a specific period, researchers can focus on trends and developments within a particular time frame, facilitating historical analyses or identifying recent advancements.
- Publication. Researchers can narrow their scope by selecting specific publications. This filter ensures that the analysis is confined to the most relevant sources.
- Model. The model filter lets scholars specify whether to include hypothesized models, empirically verified models, or both. This enables a detailed examination of theoretical proposals and their empirical validations.

- Concepts of interest. Users can pinpoint particular concepts or keywords central to their research. This filter ensures that the analysis concentrates on these specified concepts, providing deeper insights into their connections in the literature.

The selected filters are applied to the five-level analysis. Scholars have the flexibility to focus on the levels that matter most to them without having to follow a specific order. The five levels, as previously discussed, are concept, relationship, model, theme, and theory. Chapter 6 illustrates these analyses in detail and provides guidance on how to interpret the results effectively.

SUMMARY

- **Five-Level analysis framework**: A five-level analysis framework is designed to guide causal knowledge analysis, covering elements, relationships, models, themes, and theories.
- **Element level**: The focus is on the foundational building blocks of theories, such as concepts, constructs, and events, and utilizes tools such as GQL and NLP to analyze definitions and similarities.
- **Element–Relationship level**: This explores the connections between concepts and their positions in causal knowledge networks, using network science metrics and association rule mining to understand the roles and relationships of concepts.
- **Model level**: This addresses the identification of similar causal models and supports rigorous causal reasoning through graph isomorphism, NLP, and DAG theory.
- **Theory level**: This examines the frequency and influence of theories within a knowledge network, employing social network analysis to assess their impact and connectivity.
- **Theme level**: This evaluates knowledge fragmentation, convergence, and consensus within the thematic domain, providing a field-level view of the knowledge network.
- **Analysaurus app**: The Analysaurus app is a web-based application developed to facilitate CKA by providing efficient and direct access to core knowledge through five levels of analysis. The app connects

to a graph database of coded articles and allows scholars to use various filters to specify the scope of their analysis.

NOTES

1. https://t-rex-graph.org/analysaurus
2. Other transformers could be used.

6. Illustration of causal knowledge analytics

CODED PUBLICATIONS

The database for the tools in this book is a set of coded publications included in the *MIS Quarterly* (MISQ) Curations.[1] The MISQ Curations identify topics deemed of significant interest to the IS (information systems) field, and each curation includes a set of MISQ articles that are assessed by the curators as making important contributions to a topic. The 13 curations include 524 papers, of which 238 (53 percent) include an explicit causal or process model and thus are included in this database. Features of each curation are summarized in Table 6.1 and presented along with the list of papers in Appendix 4. The graph database of all curations contains 5,227 nodes and 9,500 relationships. The MISQ Curations are updated as new articles related to the topics are published.[2]

Encoded MISQ Curations papers are a suitable database for this book for the following reasons. First, each curation contains a set of papers on the same topic and builds a review-like database to demonstrate proposed review and synthesis methods. Second, these papers are considered significant and representative of a topic, as their inclusion in MISQ Curations is evaluated and decided by senior scholars familiar with the curated topic. Finally, the resulting graph database has sufficient nodes and relationships to challenge human comprehension, and it requires data analytics for a holistic understanding of the collection of causal models. One of the purposes of MISQ Curations is to provide researchers with easy access to a set of significant topics (Rai and Bush, 2018). This book provides supplementary material for the curations through digitized knowledge and the proposed analytics methods. We present here the results of causal knowledge analytics based on the codified MISQ Curations.

Table 6.1 *MISQ Curation papers*

Curation	Articles	Articles coded	Percent with causal models	Total nodes	Total edges
Health Information Technology	41	25	61	405	570
Information Privacy	26	13	50	409	690
Information Systems Alignment	29	13	44.8	247	408
Information Systems Sourcing	39	21	53.8	483	912
IS Control and Governance	53	17	32.1	407	808
IS Use	114	67	58.8	1,572	2,889
IT Project Management	39	19	48.7	478	838
IT-supported Collaboration	38	23	60.5	431	683
IT Workforce	66	31	47	634	1,132
Knowledge Management	49	24	49	527	896
Online Word-of-Mouth	31	13	41.9	178	224
Securing Digital Assets	36	16	44.4	453	782
Trust	35	28	80	919	1,796
Combined database	524	238	45.4	5,227	9,500

ELEMENT-LEVEL ANALYSIS

Element-level analysis focuses on the examination of elements utilizing GQL (graph query language) and NLP (natural language processing). Finding publications with element-centric searches avoids tangential content. Element semantic similarity indicates nuances in conceptual understanding, which is a starting point for addressing jingle and jangle issues.[3] Identifying the diverse topics associated with each element

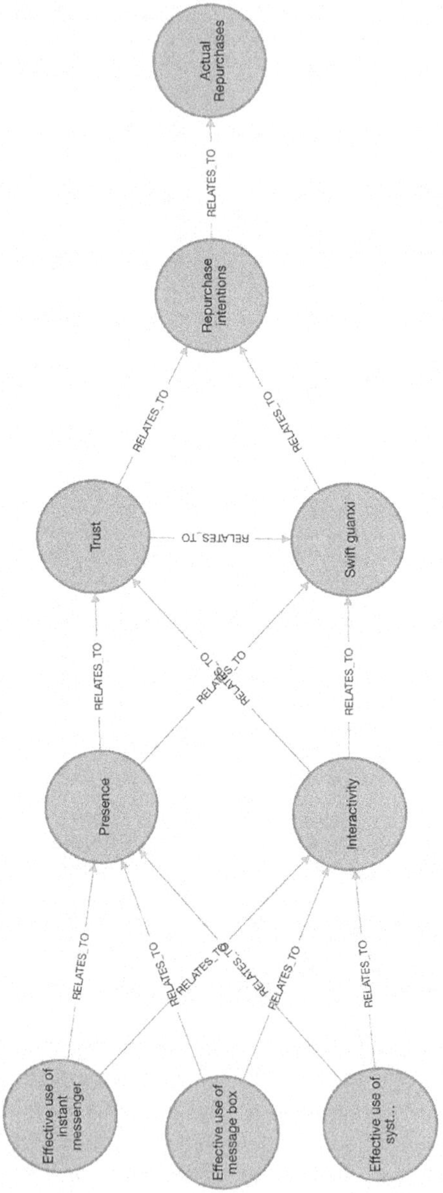

Source: Ou et al., 2014.

Figure 6.1 Research model containing Trust

reveals various perspectives from which elements are studied in the literature.

Finding publications through element-centric searches

Although concept-centric literature reviewing is widely adopted for synthesizing around a concept rather than summarizing by authors (Webster and Watson, 2002), conducting concept-centric searches using full-text search engines can result in an overly large list of articles because many tangential publications are typically included. However, a graph knowledge database enables precise searching for publications containing a specific concept in a causal model (see Table 6.2). A specific causal model can be retrieved for further investigation (Figure 6.1). Revealing the correspondence between papers and concepts provides scholars with a starting point for synthesis (Table 6.3).

Table 6.2 Publications associated with the concept Trust

Publication citation
Gefen, Karahanna, & Straub. (2003). Trust and TAM in Online Shopping: An Integrated Model. *MIS Quarterly*, 27(1), 51. DOI:10.2307/30036519
Cyr, Head, Larios, & Pan. (2009). Exploring Human Images in Website Design: A Multi-Method Approach. *MIS Quarterly*, 33(3), 539. DOI:10.2307/20650308
Xiao, & Benbasat. (2007). E-Commerce Product Recommendation Agents: Use, Characteristics, and Impact. *MIS Quarterly*, 31(1), 137. DOI:10.2307/25148784
Goo, Kishore, Rao, & Nam. (2009). The Role of Service Level Agreements in Relational Management of Information Technology Outsourcing: An Empirical Study. *MIS Quarterly*, 33(1), 119. DOI:10.2307/20650281
Pavlou, Liang, & Xue. (2007). Understanding and Mitigating Uncertainty in Online Exchange Relationships: A Principal-Agent Perspective. *MIS Quarterly*, 31(1), 105.

Computing element semantic similarity

The definition of critical concepts is vital for understanding a research report. However, concepts can be defined in various ways across articles. For example (as mentioned in Chapter 5), one review reports 23 different

Table 6.3 Concepts associated with a large number of publications

Concept	Number of publications
Perceived usefulness	10
Trust	10
Performance	8
Social presence	7
Perceived ease of use	7
Gender	7
Facilitating conditions	7
Role ambiguity	6
Behavioral intention	6
Job satisfaction	5
Satisfaction	5
Firm performance	5

definitions of "digital transformation" (Vial, 2019). Jingle and jangle fallacies highlight the importance of being aware of such definitions (Song et al., 2021).

Searching for definitions using full-text search engines requires scholars to skim many publications. However, a graph database can return definitions precisely with a query. NLP can assist scholars in comparing definitions by analyzing similarities among concepts' definitions and providing a report. As an illustration, BERT (Devlin et al., 2018) can compute the similarity of definitions in the MISQ *Trust* curation (Table 6.4). Inspection of Table 6.5 reveals that definition 3 has the highest average similarity score. The most similar definition pairs are 1 and 3, and 1 and 5 (bold), while the least similar pairs are 1 and 7, and 5 and 7 (italic). A scholar can further examine why authors adopt dissimilar definitions and then assess the consequences of their study on that concept.

Identifying topics associated with elements

Topics associated with a concept are not easily retrievable from full-text search engines as the information is not pre-identified or coded, which results in scholars manually reading and identifying them. The number of associated topics informs which concept is relevant to various

Table 6.4 *Trust definitions and source publications*

Definition number	Definition	Source publication
1	We define trust as the subjective assessment of one party that another party will perform a particular transaction according to his or her confident expectations, in an environment characterized by uncertainty.	Ba and Pavlou, 2002, p. 245
2	Trust is argued to be rooted in perceptions of teammates' ability, benevolence, and integrity. Ability refers to the aptitude and skills that enable an individual to be perceived as competent by teammates. Benevolence refers to the extent to which an individual is believed to be willing to help teammates beyond personal motives or individual gain. Integrity refers to the extent to which an individual is believed to adhere to a set of principles thought to make her dependable and reliable.	Piccoli and Ives, 2003, p. 366
3	Trust is defined as the buyer's intentions to accept vulnerability based on her beliefs that the transaction will meet her confident expectations.	Pavlou et al., 2007, p. 107
4	The user beliefs in the recommendation agents' competence, benevolence, and integrity. The beliefs that 1) the recommendation agent has the ability, skills, and expertise to perform effectively 2) the recommendation agent cares about the user and acts in the user's interest 3) the recommendation agent adheres to a set of principles (e.g., honesty and promise keeping) that the user finds acceptable.	Xiao and Benbasat, 2007, p. 144
5	Trust reflects one party's belief that its requirements will be fulfilled through future actions undertaken by the other party.	Goo et al., 2009, p. 126
6	Trust is conceptualized as a single variable and refers to general confidence in the website.	Cyr et al., 2009, p. 545
7	The extent to which a buyer perceives in a seller's ability (i.e., skills, competencies, and characteristics in seller his/her products online), integrity (adhering to a set of principles that the buyer finds acceptable), and benevolence (i.e., doing good toward the buyer).	Ou et al., 2014, p. 217

Table 6.5 *Definition similarity analysis*

Definition	**1**	**2**	**3**	**4**	**5**	**6**	**7**
1	—	—	—	—	—	—	—
2	0.6	—	—	—	—	—	—
3	**0.8**	0.63	—	—	—	—	—
4	0.57	0.76	0.63	—	—	—	—
5	**0.81**	0.61	0.77	0.57	—	—	—
6	0.59	0.5	0.57	0.49	0.46	—	—
7	*0.38*	0.57	0.52	0.76	*0.38*	0.45	—
Means	0.62	0.61	0.66	0.63	0.6	0.51	0.58

topics and phenomena. Revealing the associated topics surfaces the lens through which a concept is investigated. The number of associated curations for each concept varies from one to eight. In our example, *Trust* has been studied in eight curations, suggesting that scholars studying various phenomena find *Trust* relevant (Table 6.6). This analysis indicates that a synthesis of findings might help to consolidate knowledge or topics that could be considered from another conceptual perspective.

ELEMENT–RELATIONSHIP ANALYSIS

Elements are not isolated in the literature. Understanding elements requires studying their relationships with other elements. This section illustrates how causal knowledge analytics assists this process by retrieving related elements, identifying elements' positions in a network, and pinpointing elements with specific roles in a network (for example mediators and moderators).

Retrieving antecedents, consequents, and causal chains

Synthesizing knowledge about a concept involves learning what causes it (antecedents), what it causes (consequents), and the associated causal chains. Querying a graph database of causal models can efficiently reveal the related concepts, such as the antecedents of *Trust* (Figure 6.2), and an antecedent chain (Figure 6.3). These figures reveal a variety of causal explanations of a phenomenon.

Table 6.6 Concepts studied in multiple curations

Concept	Curations	Number of curations
Trust	Information Privacy, Trust, IS Use, IS Control and Governance, IS Sourcing, IT-supported Collaboration, IT Project Management, Online Word-of-Mouth	8
Performance	IT-supported Collaboration, IT Workforce, IS Alignment, IS Use, Knowledge Management, IS Sourcing	6
Group performance	Health Information Technology, IS Alignment, IS Use, Knowledge Management, Trust	5
Project success	IS Control and Governance, IT Project Management, IT Workforce, IS Sourcing, Trust	5
Social presence	IT-supported Collaboration, Information Privacy, Trust, Knowledge Management, Securing Digital Assets	5
Client participation	IS Control and Governance, IS Sourcing, IT Project Management, Trust	4
Cognition-based trust	IT-supported Collaboration, IT Workforce, Knowledge Management, Trust	4
Commitment	IT Workforce, IS Control and Governance, IS Sourcing, Trust	4
Expertise location	IT-supported Collaboration, IT Workforce, Knowledge Management, Trust	4
Future cognition-based trust	IT-supported Collaboration, IT Workforce, Knowledge Management, Trust	4

Identifying mediators and moderators

By pinpointing potential moderators and mediators, scholars can decide if they need to discuss them as related literature, consider including them during research model development, and examine results considering

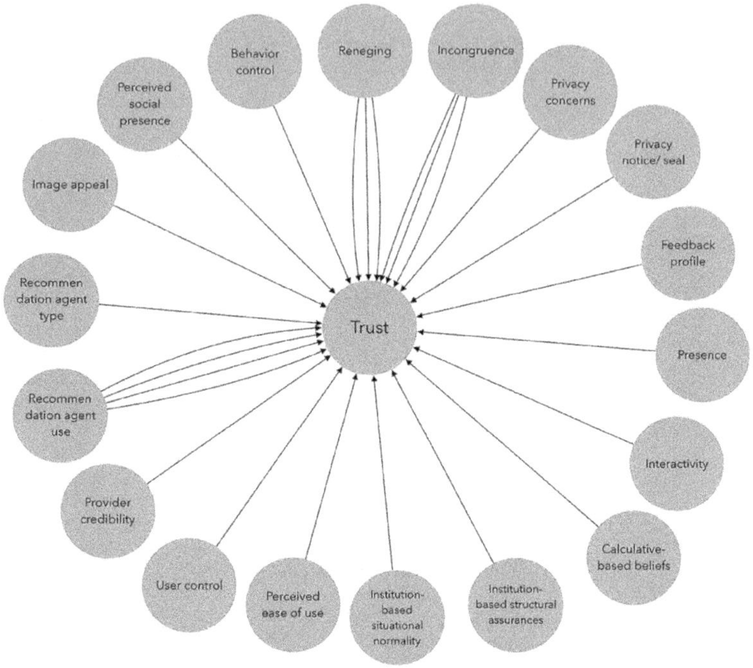

Figure 6.2 *Antecedents of Trust*

the mechanism of why and under which conditions certain effects vary. Frequent moderators and mediators in the *IS Alignment* curation are reported in Tables 6.7 and 6.8. Other utilities include querying which relationships are moderated or mediated by a concept of interest and which moderators or mediators impact a relationship.

Pinpointing peripheral concepts and publications

Learning a concept or publication's relative position in a knowledge network reveals its importance or novelty. Network measures can assist by quantifying the position of a node in the network. A peripheral node is close to the edge of a graph, and we can compute a periphery index from a node's eccentricity and its graph's diameter. The eccentricity of a node is the length of its longest shortest path to all its connected nodes

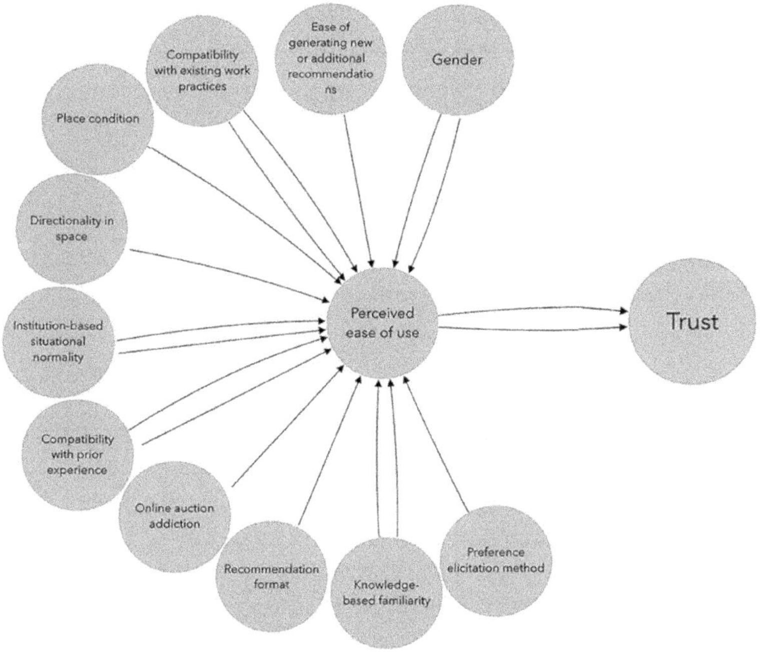

Figure 6.3 *Antecedents of an antecedent of Trust*

Table 6.7 *Moderators in the IS Alignment curation*

Moderator	**Frequency**
Culture	19
Gender	14
Mutual dependence	13
Social interaction features	12
Data management features	12
Experience	11
Age	10
Product expertise	9
Task knowledge tacitness	8

Table 6.8 Mediators in the IS Alignment curation

Mediator	Frequency
Job design characteristics	9
Work exhaustion	8
Business-process specificity	6
Organizational commitment	6
Just-in-time capabilities	5
Customer and supplier participation capabilities	5
Exploitive task adaptation	4
Exploratory task adaptation	4
Seeking social support	4

(Wasserman and Faust, 1994). The maximum eccentricity of all nodes is the diameter of a graph (Wasserman and Faust, 1994). The ratio of a node's eccentricity and a graph's diameter (periphery index) is the extent to which a node is close to the edge of a graph. A node with a periphery index equal to one is on the edge of a graph. When the periphery index is zero, indicating that eccentricity equals zero, a node is isolated and has no connection with the rest of the network.

$$periphery\ index = \frac{\text{Eccentricity}}{Diameter} \in [0,1]$$

The exemplar concepts on the edge of the database of 13 curations are reported in Table 6.9. Concepts in Table 6.9 appear in only one paper, and only three of the ten concepts are defined explicitly (i.e., Deep structure, Deep structure usage, and Project escalation. Peripheral concepts are on the edge of a knowledge network and have limited access to a large portion of the network. Future research may investigate the concepts on the edge of the graph as these concepts may deal with emerging phenomena that have not been extensively studied. IS scholars could further discover and explore the relationships involving these concepts.

Identifying central concepts

Identifying concepts having a central role is a difficult task without analytical tools because of the often overwhelming size of a literature set.

Table 6.9 Ten most peripheral concepts in database of 13 MISQ curations

Concepts	Periphery index
Organizational factors	1
Project factors	1
Psychological factors	1
Race	1
Deep structure	0.95
Deep structure usage	0.95
Organizational experiences	0.95
Project escalation	0.95
Purchasing behavior	0.95
Time resources	0.95

Several network measures can indicate if a concept has a central or prominent position in a network. High out-degree centrality (Freeman, 1978) is an indicator of popular antecedents (Verweij, 2012). High in-indegree centrality (Freeman, 1978) indicates a concept is studied many times as a dependent concept. A node with high betweenness centrality (Freeman, 1977) has a strong influence on the linkage of causal relationships.

In the 13 curations, *Trust* is a fundamental antecedent, and a commonly studied consequent, and is influential to causal flows (Table 6.10). It is prominent in multiple curations, indicating that it is studied within various contexts.

Identifying elements that unite fragmented knowledge

In a causal model network, cut-point concepts (Wasserman and Faust, 1994) connect causal models and unite fragmented knowledge (Table 6.11). A cut-point is a node whose removal results in the network breaking into two or more disconnected sub-networks. These nodes play a vital role in maintaining the structural integrity of the network by acting as bridges between different components. Cut-point analysis can identify the mediator connecting two models. For example, if we have A→B in one model and B→C in another, then B is a mediator in A→B→C.

Table 6.10 Concepts in the 13 curations with the highest network centrality measures

Betweenness centrality	**Out-degree centrality**	**In-degree centrality**
Trust	Work status	Performance
Gender	Computer self-efficacy	**Trust**
Habit	Work exhaustion	Usage
Perceived usefulness	**Trust**	Turnover intention
Satisfaction	Gender	Work exhaustion
Information privacy concerns	Role ambiguity	Job satisfaction
Behavioral intention	Information privacy concerns	Perceived usefulness
Privacy concerns	Job autonomy	IT use
Group's adoption of the technology	Perceived usefulness	Behavioral intention
Group valence toward the technology	Computer support	Quality of knowledge exchanged

Table 6.11 Cut-point concepts

Concept	**Change in the number of disconnected sub-networks**
Trust	14
Intention to adopt smart metering technology	13
Performance	11
Use of electronic markets	8
Social media use	7
Privacy concerns	6
Work status	6
Behavioral intention	6
Symbolic or substantive adoption	6
Project success	6

Finding a basket of elements

Reporting concepts that frequently occur together in a causal model suggests a possible symbiotic relationship. By treating a causal model as a basket of concepts, we can apply association rule mining (Agrawal et al., 1993). To illustrate this method, association rules are identified for the IS curations (Table 6.12). Frequency refers to the counts of directional relationships from antecedent to consequent. Support refers to the proportion of the times a concept set, including both antecedent and consequent, occurs in the database (Agrawal et al., 1993). This analysis helps scholars identify frequent co-occurrence of concepts.

Table 6.12 Association rule results in the IS Use curation

Antecedent	Consequent	Frequency	Support
Facilitating conditions	Behavioral intention	4	0.06
Experience, Facilitating conditions	Behavioral intention	4	0.04
Age, Facilitating conditions	Behavioral intention	4	0.04
Facilitating conditions, Gender	Behavioral intention	4	0.04
Age, Experience, Facilitating conditions	Behavioral intention	4	0.04
Experience, Facilitating conditions, Gender	Behavioral intention	4	0.04
Age, Facilitating conditions, Gender	Behavioral intention	4	0.04
Perceived ease of use	Perceived usefulness	3	0.06

Model-Level Analysis

Model-level analysis focuses on enabling efficient discovery of related research. Model similarity can be measured by conceptual isomorphism, which is detailed in Chapter 4. An example of two models with high isomorphism is shown in Figure 6.4.

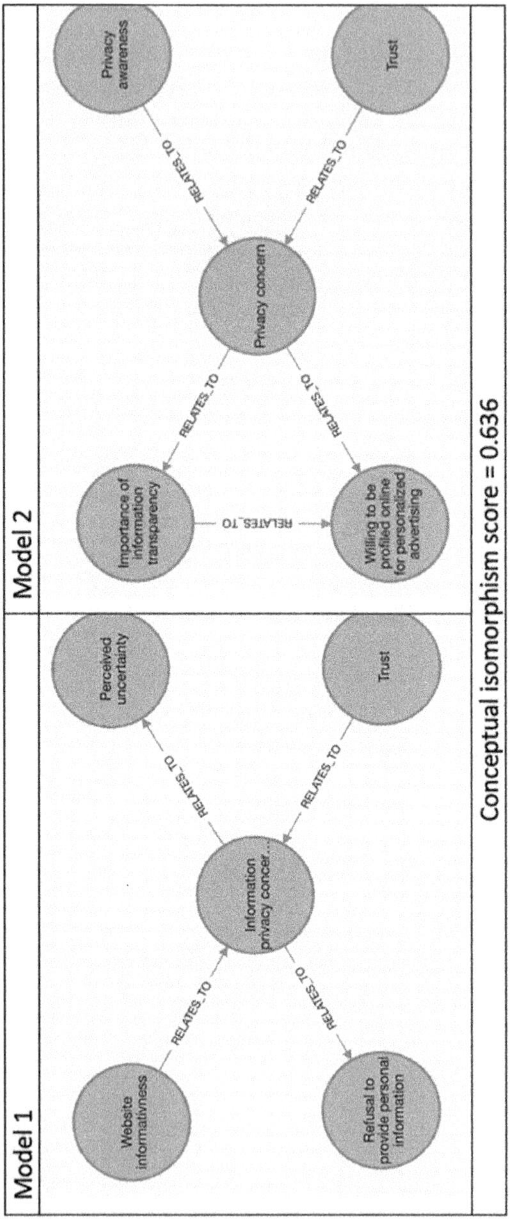

Figure 6.4 *Examples of conceptual isomorphic models*

Computing isomorphic similarity enables scholars to find similar research models to the one they are developing. It could also be valuable for reviewers when checking the extent to which a model in a manuscript under review has been studied. The method narrows down the scope of the literature that scholars need to examine closely.

We analyzed the pair-wise similarity of models and the average of model similarities in each curation (Table 6.13)[4] to assess the level of knowledge convergence. A high level of similarity among causal models indicates that scholars are investigating a topic from a similar conceptual perspective. The curations are distributed around the average level of model similarity of 0.371. *IS Alignment* and *Information Privacy* have the highest (0.434) and lowest levels (0.249) of model similarity, respectively. ANOVA shows that there are significant differences among the curations ($p<0.01$). A Tukey test (Tukey, 1949) reveals significant pair-wise differences (Figure 6.5). The average model similarity for the *IS Alignment* curation is significantly higher than most curations except

Table 6.13 *Averaged model similarity scores of 13 curations*

Curation	**Average model similarity**	**Number of models**
IS Alignment	0.434	13
Online Word-of-Mouth	0.414	13
Knowledge Management	0.404	24
IT-supported Collaboration	0.396	23
Health Information Technology	0.382	27
IT Project Management	0.378	20
IS Control and Governance	0.376	17
IS Use	0.372	68
IT Workforce	0.37	31
IS Sourcing	0.37	21
Securing Digital Assets	0.351	17
Trust	0.33	28
Information Privacy	0.249	13
Average	*0.371*	*24.2*

Note: This table is sorted by average model similarity in descending order.

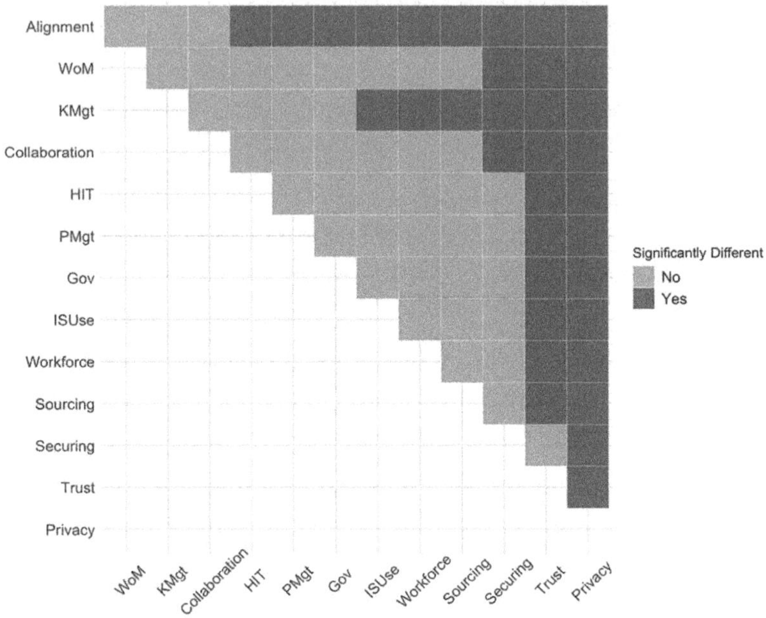

Figure 6.5 *Heat map of curation difference*

for *Online Word-of-Mouth*, *Knowledge Management*, and *IT-supported Collaboration*. The average model similarity for *Information Privacy* is significantly lower than other curations.

THEME-LEVEL ANALYSIS

Theme-level analysis enables scholars to review the literature beyond one topic and obtain a field-level view. This level of analysis informs the degree of fragmentation in knowledge networks, indicated by network connectedness, concept-topic correspondence, highly constrained elements, field-level development over time, and causal consensus in the knowledge frontier.

The level of knowledge fragmentation

Network connectivity reveals the level of accumulation and fragmentation of research topics. Concept density measures the connectivity of a network and indicates relatedness across models. High concept density indicates a greater level of convergence among scholars on concepts of interest. Low concept density suggests fragmentation. The curations *IT Workforce*, *IS Use*, and *IT-supported Collaboration* have higher concept densities than other curations (Table 6.14), suggesting that publications in these curations study similar concepts.

Table 6.14 Concept density of MISQ Curations papers

Curation	**Number of concepts**	**Concepts appearing in more than one paper**	**Concept density**
IT Workforce	147	12	0.082
IS Use	370	21	0.057
IT-supported Collaboration	120	5	0.042
IS Control and Governance	82	3	0.037
Securing Digital Assets	115	4	0.035
Information Systems Sourcing	111	3	0.027
Knowledge Management	139	3	0.022
Trust	212	4	0.019
Information Privacy	111	2	0.018
Information Systems Alignment	56	1	0.018
IT Project Management	116	2	0.017
Online Word-of-Mouth	52	0	0
Health Information Technology	114	0	0
Curation measures[5]	1250	75	0.060

Element-topic correspondence analysis

Frequently studied dependent concepts reveal the varied foci of a phenomenon. They indicate what interests a scholarly community and point to important dependent concepts. From a graph database perspective, a concept's number of incoming edges (its in-degree centrality) indicates how often it is studied as a dependent concept (see Table 6.15). The result of the correspondence analysis of curations and frequent dependent concepts is shown in Figure 6.6.

The island: The first dimension distinguishes knowledge management and knowledge-related concepts. *Knowledge Management* (J) is horizontally distant from other curations. It is closely associated with the concepts of "Quality of knowledge exchanged" (8) and "Knowledge transfer" (10). Knowledge management scholars are mainly concerned with understanding what impacts knowledge transfer.

An archipelago: Four curations – *IT Workforce* (I), *IS Alignment* (C), *IS Sourcing* (D), and *IT-supported Collaboration* (H) – are close when mapped on the horizontal axis but distant on the vertical axis. *IT*

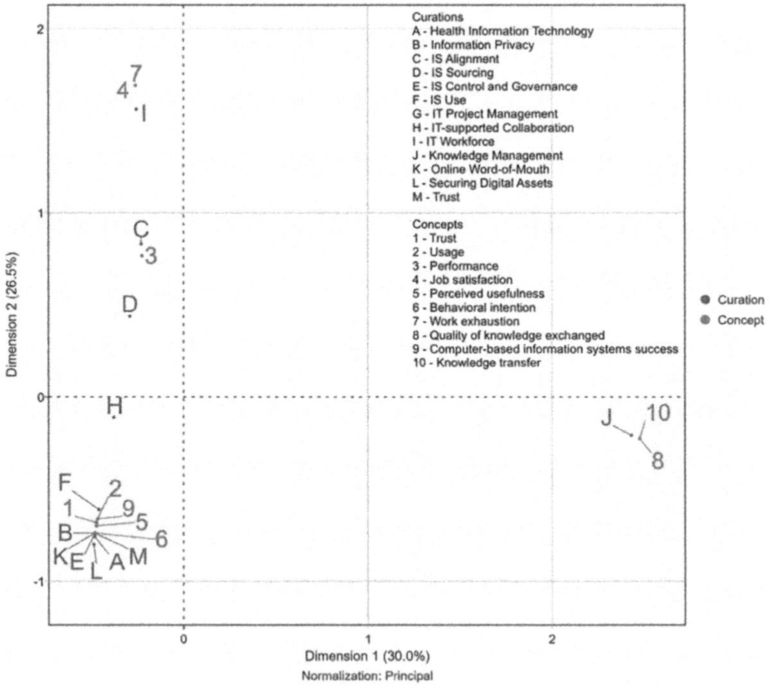

Figure 6.6 *Correspondence analysis for frequent dependent concepts by curation*

Table 6.15 Most frequently studied concepts as dependent concepts by curation

Curations	Trust	Usage	Performance	Job satisfaction	Perceived usefulness	Behavioral intention	Work exhaustion	Quality of knowledge exchanged	Computer-based IS success	Knowledge transfer	Total
Health IT	0	0	0	0	3	0	0	0	0	0	3
Information Privacy	2	0	0	0	0	0	0	0	0	0	2
IS Alignment	0	0	1	0	0	0	0	0	0	0	1
IS Sourcing	2	0	6	0	0	0	0	0	0	0	8
IS Control and Governance	5	0	0	0	0	0	0	0	0	0	5
IS Use	2	27	6	0	15	10	0	0	14	0	74
IT Project Management	0	0	0	0	0	0	0	0	0	0	0
IT-supported Collaboration	3	0	2	0	0	0	0	0	0	0	5
IT Workforce	0	0	14	22	0	0	16	0	0	0	52
Knowledge Management	0	0	1	0	0	0	0	15	0	14	30

Curations	Trust	Usage	Performance	Job satisfaction	Perceived usefulness	Behavioral intention	Work exhaustion	Quality of knowledge exchanged	Computer-based IS success	Knowledge transfer	Total
Online Word-of-Mouth	1	0	0	0	0	0	0	0	0	0	1
Securing Digital Assets	0	0	0	0	0	6	0	0	0	0	6
Trust	26	0	0	0	2	0	0	0	0	0	28
Health IT	0	0	0	0	3	0	0	0	0	0	3
Information Privacy	2	0	0	0	0	0	0	0	0	0	2
Total	43	27	30	22	23	16	16	15	14	14	220

Workforce is associated with "Job satisfaction" (4) and "Work exhaustion" (7). *IS Alignment* (C) is closely related to "Performance" (3). *IS Sourcing* (D) and *IT-supported Collaboration* (H) are not vertically close to any of the common concepts. Further investigation shows that *IS Sourcing* is primarily associated with the less-common dependent concepts of "Satisfaction with application service providers" and "Job design characteristics" (see Appendix 5). In contrast, *IT-supported Collaboration* is mainly related to "Task-knowledge coordination" and "Social presence" (Appendix 5). We interpret this group of curations as primarily, but not exclusively, concerned with IS-related dependent concepts.

A continent: The remainder of the curations and frequent dependent concepts are tightly clustered in one group. The same set of concepts is used across multiple research themes, including *Health Information Technology, IS Use, Online Word-of-Mouth, Information Privacy, Trust, IS Control and Governance*, and *Securing Digital Assets.* The common concepts are "Trust", "Usage", "Perceived usefulness", "Behavioral intention", and "Computer-based IS success". This grouping might identify the mainstream of IS research, where scholars have settled on a common set of concepts to study multiple phenomena.

IT Project Management is not shown in the results because its row sums to zero. This curation deals with concepts that are different from the others, focusing on project success. More details of this analysis are available in Appendix 5.

Identifying highly constrained elements and potential brokers

Constraint and effective size indicate the extent to which a node is constrained by its connections and its chance to access structure holes and become a broker in a network (Burt, 1992). The structural hole measure, in the causal model context, informs which concepts might have not-yet-discovered connections with other concepts and therefore are prospective research topics.

Missing links in a concept relationship network (structural holes) can indicate potential research questions. Structural holes are indicated by the measurement of constraint and effective size (Burt, 1992). Concepts with low constraint and high effective size have more access to structural holes and are more likely to be brokers and connect with other concepts. The two measures can help identify highly constrained concepts and potential brokers.

We conduct two analyses of structural holes. In both, we divide the database into two parts: causal models published between 1980 and 2000 (t1) and between 2001 and 2020 (t2) and compute the constraint, effective size, and degree (that is, the number of relationships) of each node at both time periods. For the first analysis, we are interested in the percentage of concepts in t1 that also appear in t2. We find that concepts with low constraint or high effective size in t1 have a higher likelihood of being studied in t2 (Table 6.16).

Table 6.16 Constraint and effective size measures (percentages of concepts in both time periods)

Concept structural hole measure	Number of concepts	Percentage of concepts also appearing at t2
Low constraint at t1	98	16.3%
High constraint at t1	106	10.4%
Low effective size at t1	114	11.4%
High effective size at t1	90	15.6%

Note: The average constraint and effective sizes at t1 are 0.7 and 1.9, respectively.

In the second analysis, we focus on the overlapping concepts of both time periods and calculate the average number of connections that concepts have in t2. The result shows that concepts with low constraint or high effective size in t1 have a higher degree in t2 (Table 6.17). Our findings

Table 6.17 Constraint and effective size measures (average degrees at second time period)

Concept structural hole measure	Number of concepts	Average degree at t2
Low constraint at t1	16	5.8
High constraint at t1	11	2.7
Low effective size at t1	18	3.5
High effective size at t1	9	6.7

suggest that concepts with low constraints and high effective size are less prone to obsolescence during the process of field advancement and that concepts with high constraints and low effective size are more likely to build new connections, which are consistent with structural hole theory. The finding supports the utility of structural hole measures in the causal model context and could identify highly saturated concepts or potential brokers.

Knowledge development

To understand the progression of knowledge accumulation, we report concepts with the highest effective sizes during four periods (Table 6.18).

Table 6.18 Concepts with highest effective sizes in each period

1980–1990	1991–2000	2001–2010	2011–2020
Computer-based information systems success	Use of electronic markets	Trust	Intention to adopt smart metering technology
Anonymity	Computer self-efficacy	Satisfaction	Privacy concerns
Discipline severity	Work exhaustion	Perceived usefulness	Social media use
Outcome	Gender	Perceived ease of use	Protection motivation
Process	Interaction process	Information privacy concerns	Optimal publisher website price
Group decision support system	Utilization	Behavioral intention	Symbolic or substantive adoption
Role ambiguity	Performance	Information security awareness	Desires
Role conflict	Usage	Controllability of purchasing	Performance
Group internal environment	Appropriation moves	Work exhaustion	User privacy concerns
Identification of offenders	Clarifying the magnitude of a problem	Work status	Trust

The result shows continuing shifts of research focus in the field. The field moved from studying the success and outcome of group support systems to more diverse issues, such as privacy, security, and trust.

We examine publications published in two time periods (t1: 1980–2000, and t2: 2001–2020). Concept effective size change (effective size at t2 minus that at t1) shows the research attention that the ten concepts gained between 2000 and 2020 (Table 6.19).

Table 6.19 Concepts with highest effective size changes

Concepts	**Effective size change**
Perceived usefulness	14.09
Perceived ease of use	12.65
Gender	9.45
Performance	9.27
Culture	7.88
Facilitating conditions	7.27
Decision quality	6.67
Social presence	6
Job satisfaction	5.8
Behavioral intention	5.42

Causal consensus

Assessing the level of agreement helps in understanding a topic's knowledge frontier. We identify three types of causal consensus to capture the extent to which the literature collectively agrees (the causal consensus index, CCI) regarding dependent concepts (that is, dependent concept consensus), antecedents (antecedent consensus), and consequents (consequent consensus). Figure 6.7a and 6.7b shows examples of high and low CCI.

Overall, all curations have a low level of dependent concept consensus (Table 6.20), indicating that the publications study various phenomena. A Tukey test (Tukey, 1949) shows that the antecedent consensus index of the *Heath Information Technology* curation is significantly different

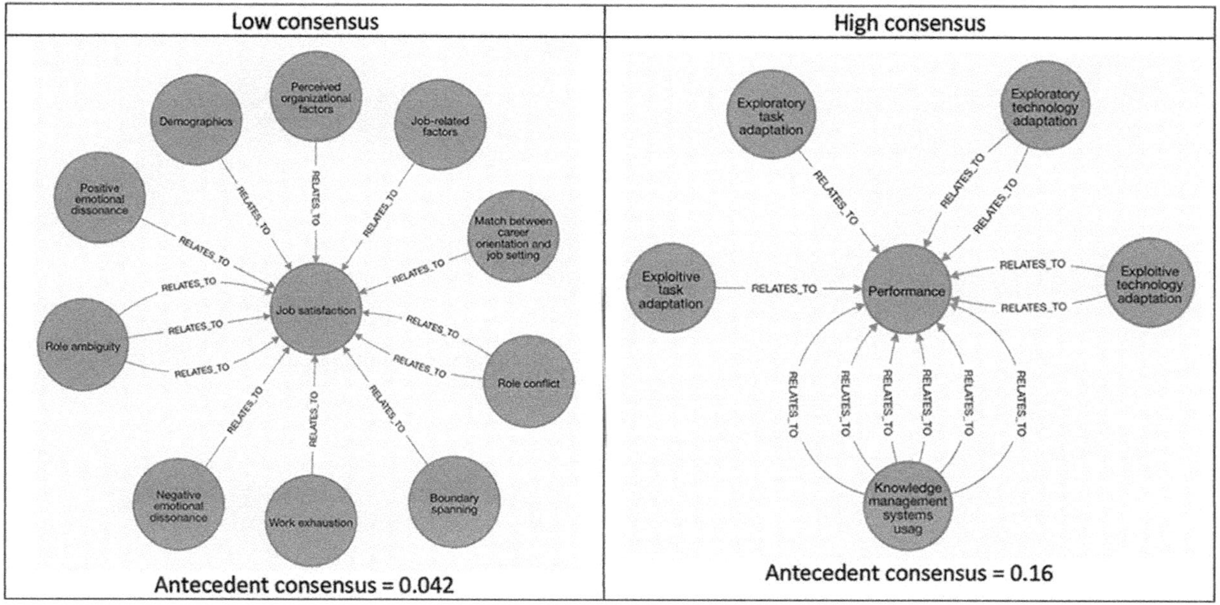

Figure 6.7a *Causal consensus index examples*

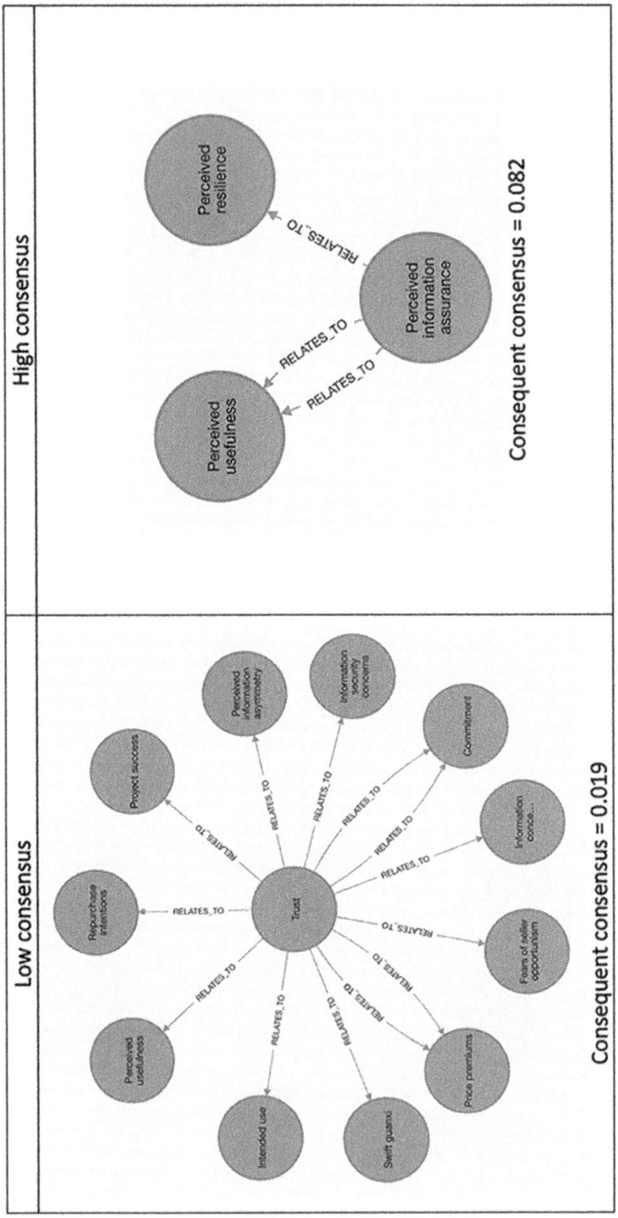

Figure 6.7b *Causal consensus index examples*

Table 6.20 Causal consensus index for each curation

Curation	Consequent consensus index	Antecedent consensus index	Dependent concept consensus index
Health Information Technology	0.909	0.686	0
Information Privacy	0.681	0.382	0
IS Alignment	0.567	0.535	0.025
IS Sourcing	0.745	0.474	0.003
IS Control and Governance	0.635	0.477	0.015
IS Use	0.714	0.467	0.015
IT Project Management	0.681	0.385	0.003
IT-supported Collaboration	0.661	0.62	0.018
IT Workforce	0.617	0.562	0.022
Knowledge Management	0.721	0.513	0.003
Online Word-of-Mouth	0.88	0.745	0
Securing Digital Assets	0.74	0.508	0
Trust	0.652	0.388	0.007
Average	0.691	0.519	0.009

from that of the *Trust* curation, while the remaining curation pairs have no significant difference. Regarding the consequent consensus index, the *Heath Information Technology* curation is significantly higher than the *IS Alignment*, *IT workforce*, and *Trust* curations. There is no significant difference for the other curation pairs.

The distribution of antecedent and consequent consensus index (Figure 6.8) shows that the *Trust*, *IT Project Management*, and *Information Privacy* curations have low antecedent consensus. The consequent consensus index in the *IS Alignment* curation is lower than in other curations. The *Health Information Technology* and *Online Word-of-Mouth*

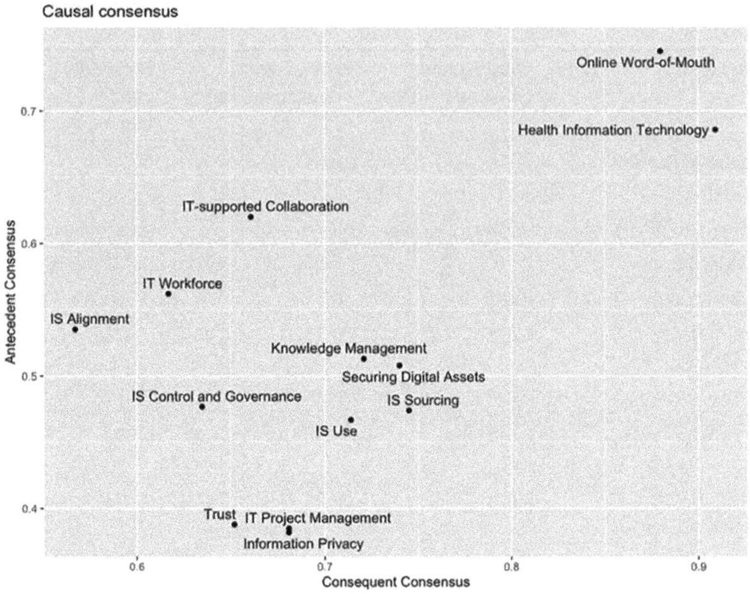

Figure 6.8 Curation causal consensus index distribution

curations have higher antecedent and consequent consensus indexes than other curations.

THEORY-LEVEL ANALYSIS

Theories guide new knowledge generation and reconceptualization of existing knowledge. Learning how theories are distributed across curations can help scholars understand the extent of their applicability to the general field of IS (Table 6.21). Scholars can visualize the theoretical foundation of various topics by using correspondence analysis, which shows that theories are split into three clusters (Figure 6.9). The first group includes agency theory (1), theory of planned behavior (2), prospect theory (5), and relational exchange theory (6). They correlate closely with the curations of *IS Control and Governance* (C), *Project Management* (J), *IS Sourcing* (E), and *Information pPrivacy* (I). The second group includes adaptive structuration theory (3), institutional theory (4), social presence theory (8), and structuration theory (9). The closely

Table 6.21 Ten most common theories in the MISQ Curations

Theory	Curations	Number of curations
Agency theory	IS Control and Governance; IS Sourcing; Information Privacy; IT Project Management; Trust	5
Theory of planned behavior	IS Control and Governance; IT Workforce; IT Project Management; Securing Digital Assets; Trust	5
Adaptive structuration theory	IT-supported Collaboration; Health Information Technology; IS Use; Trust	4
Institutional theory	Health Information Technology; IS Sourcing; IS Use; Securing Digital Assets	4
Prospect theory	IS Control and Governance; IT Workforce; Information Privacy; IT Project Management	4
Relational exchange theory	IS Control and Governance; IS Sourcing; IT Project Management; Trust	4
Social exchange theory	IS Sourcing; IT Workforce; Knowledge Management; Trust	4
Social presence theory	IT-supported Collaboration; IS Use; Information Privacy; Trust	4
Structuration theory	IS Alignment; IT-supported Collaboration; Health Information Technology; IS Use	4
Theory of reasoned action	IS Use; Knowledge Management; Securing Digital Assets; Trust	4

related curations are *IS Alignment* (A), *IT-supported Collaboration* (B), *Health Information Technology* (D), and *IS Use* (F). The third group is made up of theories that are in the middle, between groups, and do not relate closely to any curations.

An UpSet plot further reveals the intersection among curations (Figure 6.10). This figure shows: (1) a set of theories; (2) the frequency of the theories (the horizontal bars); (3) the set of theories co-occurring in publications (the matrix); and (4) their co-occurring frequency (the vertical

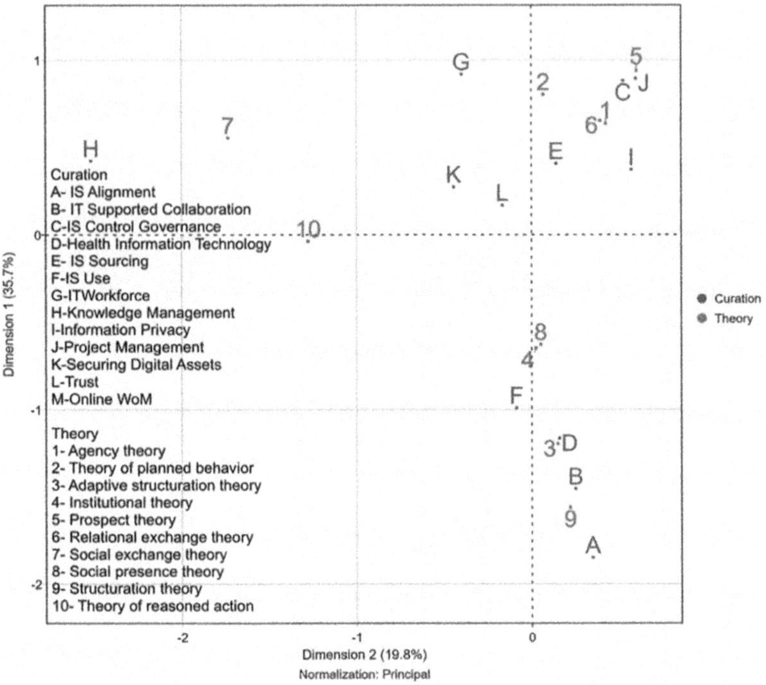

Figure 6.9 Theory–curation correspondence analysis results

bars). The most frequently used theories in the curation dataset are institutional, protection motivation, and agency theories. The paper applying four theories (the first column in the matrix) provides a unified model of information security policy compliance (Moody et al., 2018). Only three papers utilize more than one theory, which shows that theories are mainly studied independently, indicating limited theory unification. Six papers, for example, rely solely on agency theory.

A SYNTHESIS OF THE FIELD

We identify three meaningful themes for synthesizing causal knowledge analytics results: 1) curation convergence, 2) the fragmentation of the current state of knowledge, and 3) knowledge evolution (Table 6.22). An analysis based on MISQ Curations might not generalize to the IS field;

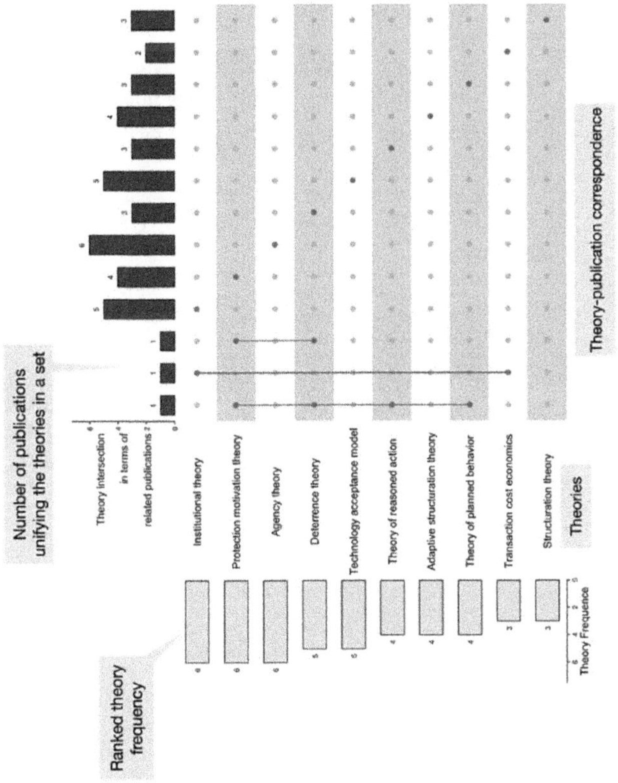

Figure 6.10 *Theories in the MISQ Curations publications*

Table 6.22 Synthesis framework of causal knowledge analytics

Theme	Question	Causal knowledge analytics task
Convergence	How do topics converge in terms of dependent concepts?	Topic–concept correspondence analysis
Convergence	How do topics converge in terms of theories studied?	Topic–theory correspondence analysis
Fragmentation	What is the level of causal consensus?	Assessing causal consensus using information theory
Fragmentation	What is the level of concept density?	Concept density analysis
Evolutionary progress	How do concept definitions evolve over time?	Concept semantic similarity analysis
Evolutionary progress	What are the concepts holding essential positions in the network in a period?	Concept network position analysis based on centrality
Evolutionary progress	What are the extensively studied concepts in a period?	Concept network position analysis based on effective size

however, it does provide a starting point for synthesizing other knowledge repositories and reproducible analytics to apply to other datasets.

Convergence

The curations converge in the following aspects. First, the curation and dependent concept correspondence analysis (see Figure 6.6) reveals that seven curations cluster together (*Health Information Technology, Information Privacy, IS Control and Governance, IS Use, Online Word-of-Mouth, Securing Digital Assets,* and *Trust*), indicating that these topics study similar dependent concepts. Second, a correspondence analysis of theory by curation posits two clusters (see Figure 6.9). One cluster includes *IS Control and Governance* (C), *Project Management* (J), *IS Sourcing* (E), and *Information Privacy* (I). The second grouping includes *IS Alignment* (A), *IT-supported Collaboration* (B), *Health Information*

Technology (D), and *IS Use* (F). The IS field examines different phenomena and technologies with similar theoretical foundations and common dependent concepts.

Fragmentation

While the synthesis shows convergence in the theoretical foundation and frequent dependent concepts, fragmentation manifests in several ways. First, the dependent concept consensus analysis shows that each curation studies a variety of dependent concepts. There is little unanimity on which outcome concepts to investigate for each topic. Second, a concept density of 0.38, for example, implies that 62 percent of concepts appear in only one paper, which is another indicator of fragmentation. These findings could be interpreted in two ways. First, the IS field has not established a core conceptual foundation that guides much research. Alternatively, the vibrancy of new technology requires a changing conceptual landscape to understand emergent phenomena.

Evolutionary progress

Causal knowledge analytics reveals the trajectory of knowledge development in the curation papers. First, concepts with the highest effective size vary in different periods (see Table 6.18). From 1980 to 1990, *Computer-based information systems success* and *Group decision support systems* were popular concepts. The research emphasis shifted in the following decade when the *Use of electronic markets* became popular. After 2000, *Social media use*, *Trust*, and privacy-related concepts received extensive attention from the community. Second, effective size shifts indicate the most intensively studied concepts during a period (see Table 6.19). From 2000 to 2020, the two concepts studied most were *Perceived usefulness* and *Perceived ease of use*. The findings highlight the evolving nature of research focus in the IS field as technology developments open up new areas for research. Another interpretation is that the field has not established an enduring conceptual foundation that is technology-invariant: it is driven by technological change rather than by fundamental questions about information systems.

NOTES

1. https://misq.org/research-curations

2. The dataset described here is up to date as of September 2021.
3. Jingle and jangle fallacies occur when two concepts with identical names reference different real-world phenomena (Thorndike, 1904), or when two identical or very similar concepts are labelled differently (Kelley, 1927).
4. We used the accurate algorithm for the calculation of graph edit distance with the time-out setting of five minutes per pair of models.
5. The combined database measures are not the sum of all curation measures as there are duplicate papers across curations.

7. The future of causal knowledge analytics

BOUNDARY

Research projects develop and evolve within boundaries. A reasonable set of boundaries keeps the projects from scope creep. In this section, we discuss the boundaries of this book. First, the coding framework captures a minimal yet useful set of components in publications. Admittedly, a more comprehensive set of data could be more informative. However, it would significantly elongate the time needed to demonstrate utility. Future research can expand the coding framework and include empirical data, concept measurement, and so on.

Coding was done manually to ensure data quality. Machines cannot recognize and extract knowledge as accurately as humans, as illustrated by the failure of IBM's Watson Health project (discussed in Chapter 2), which intended to extract medical knowledge using machine learning methods. Since the ultimate goal is knowledge analytics, high-quality data is essential. The primary goal of this book is to develop causal knowledge analytics and demonstrate what could be done with coded knowledge. Future research can explore the possibility of utilizing AI and machine learning methods in the coding process. One possible direction is to train machines on human-coded data and improve accuracy.

Causal knowledge analytics is a methodology to shorten the time needed for scholars to reach the knowledge frontier. While CKA empowers scholars to process codified literature, it does not obviate the need to interpret and integrate the results. We expect that making sense of findings will develop in profundity as more scholars become engaged in interpreting the output of different methods. They will also need to integrate non-digitized knowledge into their synthesis. These combined efforts will be central to conceptualizing and reconceptualizing knowledge.

IMPLICATION

Decades ago, scholars were reliant on physical copies of publications to disseminate and access knowledge. The advent of PDF technologies allows journals and scholars to digitize documents and significantly improve knowledge accessibility. Google Scholar has taken this advancement a step further by establishing a comprehensive repository of digital publications, facilitating keyword-based searches, and interconnecting publications through citations. However, knowledge dissemination and acquisition face significant challenges due to the exponentially expanding knowledge base. There is a critical and urgent need for a new generation of theoretical frameworks and information systems designed to enhance scholarly productivity. Such systems should digitize core knowledge, give scholars direct access to core knowledge, and facilitate knowledge engineering and analytics.

The value of digitization and analytics is prominently exemplified in industry. The relational model and SQL were developed decades ago to release organizational employees from the tedium of shuffling through filing cabinets for data. Then, relational database technology facilitated the development of data analytics. The same profound revolution hardly touched scholarship. We failed to digitize our knowledge, resulting in a consequent slowdown in scholarly productivity and discovery. Digitization has been the great driver of business productivity growth, and there is every reason to posit a similar effect to be had on scholarly productivity. We envision that the techniques proposed in this book can apply to social science in general, where causal models are common expressions of knowledge. This is an opportunity for the IS community to lead the social sciences and pioneer the development of standardized knowledge digitization and causal knowledge analytics. Few organizations can prosper without digitizing their data and using analytics to improve decision-making. It is time for scholars to emulate business, take the digitization path, and escalate the insights of analytics.

Causal knowledge analytics accelerates the process of reaching the knowledge frontier and enhances scholarly productivity. First, it accelerates searching. For instance, querying a graph database can efficiently and precisely return definitions of concepts, show which articles examine the impact of A on B, and identify which concepts are studied as mediators or moderators. Second, it assists scholars in synthesizing research. A graph database of causal models defragments knowledge and connects models in individual papers. A search can return results from a literature set, such as all the antecedents of a concept. Third, CKA can suggest new research areas. For instance, peripheral concepts and related causal models could contain innovative ideas worth developing. Structural hole measures can pinpoint concepts that have not been extensively studied yet. Fourth, it can reveal the trajectory of knowledge progression, such as how concepts' definitions, central and peripheral concepts, and research themes change and evolve. The analytical techniques introduced in this book are a start to developing causal knowledge analytics, and the presented five-level framework provides a helpful reference for future development.

The focus on causal models does not rule out the applicability of coding other types of publication, such as process models or other types of research. For instance, theories derived from qualitative work could be recorded. Coding the current state of knowledge does not neglect the past, because knowledge creation is cumulative, and new knowledge builds on its legacy work. Other approaches, such as literature review articles or PhD dissertations, could code knowledge and build a knowledge repository collectively. Future research can also look into how machines can assist the coding process in an accurate and consistent manner.

INSTITUTIONALIZATION OF KNOWLEDGE CODIFICATION

Coding papers by a third party is not a long-term solution. A viable solution, instead, is to institutionalize publication codification by journals making it obligatory where relevant. Authors have the most expertise in their work and, therefore, are the most appropriate candidates for the coding task. If journals adopt this approach and mandate coding, authors will comply and collectively build a digitized knowledge database. The peer-review process can ensure the quality of publication coding, which can be stored as a QR code attached to publications (Hung et al., 2019). Libraries, as knowledge repositories, are appropriate hosts for knowledge graphs consisting of coded articles. The AIS eLibrary,[1] for instance, could store the codes and digitized causal models of published articles and conference proceedings.

Innovation comes with operational adjustments. For example, the shift from horse carriages to automobiles required infrastructure changes such as gas stations and highways, but vehicles have enabled humans to travel greater distances at much higher speeds. Comparatively, the cost of institutionalization of core knowledge digitization in social sciences is much less significant, yet the gain in scholarly productivity would be substantial. Coding a publication with Codasaurus takes roughly 10 to 15 minutes, and it is a minimal addition to the peer-review and publication process. Conferences provide a good starting point for this initiative. By implementing codification at conferences, academic communities can pilot the process, refine it based on feedback, and gradually expand it to include journal publications. This phased approach offers a smooth transition to a digitized knowledge system.

FUTURE RESEARCH

This book pioneers the research conversation on causal knowledge analytics by establishing a coding standard, building a five-level analytics framework, and providing exemplar analyses at each level. Several future research directions are identified that can build on this book. First, ConceptNet (similar to WordNet, discussed in Chapter 4) can be developed to link and group concepts based on various types of proximity, such as semantic similarity, co-occurrences in publications or segments of publications (for example a section), and structural similarity in causal model networks. LLMs and NLP can process text fields in causal model graph databases and PDFs of publications to identify concept occurrence. Graph similarity measures can indicate the closeness of concepts in terms of their positions in knowledge networks. Another potentially fruitful research direction is to explore where AI methods and CKA excel in processing the literature and how to utilize the two research methods in a complementary fashion. With more causal models coded, machine learning methods can be used to interpret and predict a causal model network. For instance, link prediction methods can be trained on coded models to predict what relationships among concepts might be established in future research. Clustering algorithms can potentially identify groups of concepts, indicating research streams in the literature. Finance research is exploring the possibility of extracting causal models from data using AI methods (see, for example, Sokolov et al., 2024). Measures developed in this book can be utilized to analyze the societal impact of extracted causal models.

More research potential will be discovered as this stream of research evolves and matures. We need the social science community to collectively and collaboratively contribute to developing causal knowledge analytics to transform scholarly productivity.

SUMMARY

- **Research boundaries**: Establishing clear research boundaries prevents scope creep. The coding framework proposed in this book focuses on essential publication components. Future research can expand to include empirical data and concept measurement. Manual coding ensures high data quality, which is crucial for effective knowledge analytics.
- **Institutionalizing knowledge codification**: Coding by a third party is unsustainable. Journals should mandate or at least encourage coding by authors and ensure quality through reviewers, who have the most expertise in their work. This institutional approach would create a collective digitized knowledge database.
- **Implications for scholarly productivity**: Digitization and analytics, as seen in industry, have not fully impacted scholarly productivity. There is an urgent need for new information systems to digitize core knowledge, facilitate direct access, and enhance knowledge engineering and analytics. These advancements could significantly boost scholarly productivity.
- **Future research directions**: This book establishes a foundation for causal knowledge analytics. Future research could develop ConceptNet to link and group concepts, explore the complementary use of AI and CKA in literature processing, and predict causal model networks using machine learning. The social science community's collective effort is essential for advancing CKA and transforming scholarly productivity.

NOTE

1. https://aisnet.org/page/AISeLibrary

Appendix 1

CODING GUIDANCE AND SAMPLE CYPHER CODE FOR A PUBLICATION

This appendix provides guidance on creating a graph of a causal or process model using a GDL. First, we create nodes and specify their properties. We use the element "Actual repurchases" as an example:[1]

```
CREATE (:Element {elementName: "Repurchase intentions", elementType: "Construct"})
```

CREATE is used to specify nodes. A node's label is defined using a colon, *:Element*. Properties of a node are added using key-value pairs. These rules are generalizable to create other types of node. In this example, the node is labeled as Element and has two properties: elementName is "Repurchase intention" and elementType is "Construct". Second, we create relationships among nodes. We use the "Has" relationships between Relation and Element as an example:

```
MATCH (a:Relation {number:4}), (b:Element {elementName:"Repurchase intentions"}), (c:Element {elementName:"Actual repurchases"})
CREATE (a)-[r1:HAS{role :"antecedent"}]->(b)
CREATE (a)-[r2:HAS{role :"consequent"}]->(c)
RETURN r1, r2;
```

The *MATCH ... CREATE ...* statement creates relationships between nodes. The *MATCH* clause specifies the involved nodes (Element "Actual repurchases", Element "Repurchase intentions", and a Relation node). The syntax for creating relationships and specifying relationships between nodes is generalizable to other types of relationship. In this example, "Actual repurchases" and "Repurchase intentions" are connected via the relation node with a property of antecedent and consequent, correspondingly (Figure A1.1).

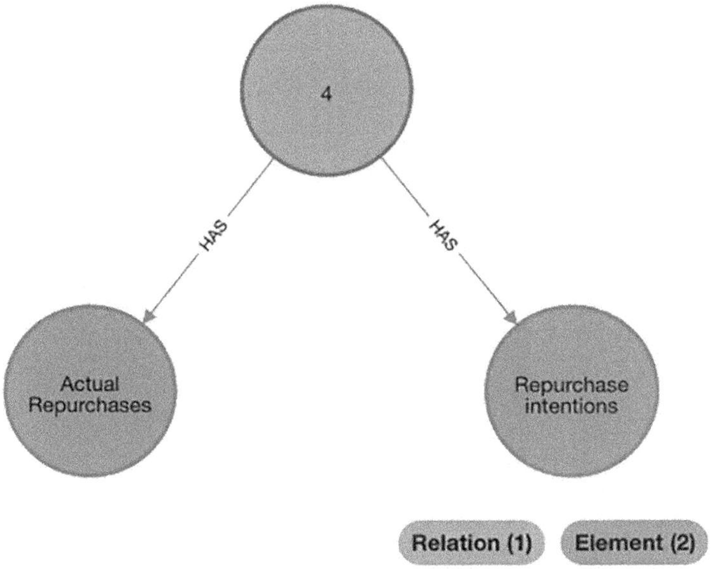

Source: Song et al., 2024.

Figure A1.1 Neo4j implementation of element relationships

Constraints should be defined when a graph database is initially created to avoid duplicate entries and ensure information retrieval accuracy. For example, we add constraints on elements' and definitions' names, publications' DOIs or ISBNs, and authors' ORCIDs to ensure a node's identifier is unique. We suggest adding the following constraints when creating a database.

```
CREATE constraint on (a:Element) ASSERT a.elementName is unique;
CREATE constraint on (a:Definition) ASSERT a.uuid is unique;
CREATE constraint on (a:Definition) ASSERT a.definition is unique;
CREATE constraint on (a:Publication) ASSERT a.DOI is unique;
CREATE constraint on (a:Publication) ASSERT a.ISBN is unique;
CREATE constraint on (a:Publication) ASSERT a.uuid is unique;
CREATE constraint on (a:Author) ASSERT a.ORCID is unique;
CREATE constraint on (a:Author) ASSERT a.uuid is unique;
CREATE constraint on (a:Theory) ASSERT a.theoryTitle is unique;
```

```
CREATE constraint on (a:Model) ASSERT a.uuid is unique;
CREATE constraint on (a:Relation) ASSERT a.uuid is unique;
```

The following is sample code for the publication (Ou et al., 2014).

```
// Author: Yuanyuan (April) Song
// CREATE constraint on (a:Element) ASSERT a.elementName is unique;
CREATE constraint on (a:Definition) ASSERT a.uuid is unique;
CREATE constraint on (a:Definition) ASSERT a.definition is unique;
CREATE constraint on (a:Publication) ASSERT a.DOI is unique;
CREATE constraint on (a:Publication) ASSERT a.ISBN is unique;
CREATE constraint on (a:Publication) ASSERT a.uuid is unique;
CREATE constraint on (a:Author) ASSERT a.ORCID is unique;
CREATE constraint on (a:Author) ASSERT a.uuid is unique;
CREATE constraint on (a:Theory) ASSERT a.theoryTitle is unique;
CREATE constraint on (a:Model) ASSERT a.uuid is unique;
CREATE constraint on (a:Relation) ASSERT a.uuid is unique;
//Create a publication with properties for DOI (document object uuidentifier)
and the citation.
CREATE (:Publication {DOI: '10.25300/misq/2014/38.1.10', citation: "Ou, C.
X.,Pavlou,P.A.,&Davison,R.M.(2014).SwiftGuanxiinOnlineMarketplaces:
TheRoleofComputer-MediatedCommunicationTechnologies.MISQuarterly,
38(1), 209–230.",uuid:"8959ebba-fbfc-4fc1–9705–64042206557f"});
// Create each element with a property of elementName and elementType
CREATE (:Element {elementName: 'Actual Repurchases', elementType:
'Construct'});
CREATE (:Element {elementName: 'Repurchase intentions', elementType:
'Construct'});
CREATE (:Element {elementName: 'Swift guanxi', elementType:
'Construct'});
CREATE (:Element {elementName: 'Trust', elementType: 'Construct'});
CREATE (:Element {elementName: 'Presence', elementType: 'Construct'});
CREATE (:Element {elementName: 'Interactivity', elementType:
'Construct'});
CREATE (:Element {elementName: 'Effective use of instant messenger',
elementType: 'Construct'});
CREATE (:Element {elementName: 'Effective use of message box', element-
Type: 'Construct'});
CREATE (:Element {elementName: 'Effective use of feedback system', ele-
mentType: 'Construct'});
// Create definitions of constructs and concepts
CREATE(:Definition{DefinitionName:'ActualRepurchases',definition:"The
frequency of actual re-transactions that a buyer conducted with a focal online
seller.",uuid:"9be6d484–1187–4997–9a79–6784311e669b"});
CREATE (:Definition {DefinitionName: 'Repurchase intentions',
definition:"A buyer's perceived likelihood of a re-transaction with a focal
online seller.",uuid:"534c33cd-9c2f-438b-b5f7-b5c1e89b1aa3"});
```

CREATE (:Definition {DefinitionName: 'Swift guanxi', definition:"A buyer's perception of a quickly formed relationship with a seller that consists of (1) mutual understanding (appre- ciating each other's needs), (2) relationship harmony (respect and conflict avouuidance), and (3) reciprocal favor (positive benefits based on each other's kind actions) in the context of online marketplaces.",uuid:"9f62df02-e181–47e5–8108–6b4e2e9bcfbb"});
CREATE (:Definition {DefinitionName: 'Trust', definition:"The extent to which a buyer perceives in a seller's ability (i.e., skills, competencies, and characteristics in seller his/her products online), integrity (adhering to a set of principles that the buyer finds acceptable), and benevolence (i.e., doing good toward the buyer).",uuid:"02924d1f-7915–4aae-ab56–8b234d24af56"});
CREATE (:Definition {DefinitionName: 'Presence', definition:"The extent to which a buyer perceives the immediacy (i.e., physical distance) and intimacy (i.e., psychological distance) between a buyer and a seller. Presence includes telepresence (which refers to a buyer's perception of being present at a seller's location remote from the buyer's own location) and social presence (which refers to a buyer's perception of intimacy with a seller in terms of human contact, human warmth and sensitivity).",uuid:"8caedfb2–4158–44a0-a617–3f8e1c34e2af"});
CREATE (:Definition {DefinitionName: 'Interactivity', definition:"The extent to which a buyer perceives that the interaction with the seller can be actively controlled and the degree to which the communication is synchronized. Interactivity thus encompasses active control (the degree of active control parties have over the communication process), two-way communication (the extent to which the communication is reciprocal), and synchronicity (the degree to which their communication is synchronized).",uuid:"5285a31c-f1d3-–4bf6-b6d8–07d8e84c2360"});
CREATE (:Definition {DefinitionName: 'Effective use of instant messenger', definition:"The extent to which a buyer believes that the effective use of the embedded Instant Messenger tool in the online marketplace can facilitate a communication among buyers and sellers.",uuid:"938d35cc-a8bd-4df9-8037-3fd199ede4d0"});
CREATE (:Definition {DefinitionName: 'Effective use of message box', definition:"The extent to which a buyer believes that the effective use of the embedded message box in the online market- place can facilitate a communication among buyers and sellers.",uuid:"5d2f4521–73c8–4660–89a3–3153d4abb271"});
CREATE (:Definition {DefinitionName: 'Effective use of feedback system', definition:"The extent to which a buyer believes that the effective use of the embedded feedback system in the online marketplace can facilitate a communication among buyers and sellers.",uuid: "1c881ca3–61da-4c8a-8b6b-b3ee8e6c3323"});
// Create relationships between a publication and definitions it contains
MATCH (p:Publication {uuid:"8959ebba-fbfc-4fc1–9705–64042206557f"}),
(a:Definition {uuid: '9be6d484–1187–4997–9a79–6784311e669b'})
CREATE (p)-[r:DEFINES]->(a)
RETURN r;

```
MATCH (p:Publication {uuid:"8959ebba-fbfc-4fc1–9705–64042206557f"}),
(a:Definition {uuid: '534c33cd-9c2f-438b-b5f7-b5c1e89b1aa3'})
CREATE (p)-[r:DEFINES]->(a)
RETURN r;
MATCH (p:Publication {uuid:"8959ebba-fbfc-4fc1–9705–64042206557f"}),
(a:Definition {uuid: '9f62df02-e181–47e5–8108–6b4e2e9bcfbb'})
CREATE (p)-[r:DEFINES]->(a)
RETURN r;
MATCH (p:Publication {uuid:"8959ebba-fbfc-4fc1–9705–64042206557f"}),
(a:Definition {uuid: '02924d1f-7915–4aae-ab56–8b234d24af56'})
CREATE (p)-[r:DEFINES]->(a)
RETURN r;
MATCH (p:Publication {uuid:"8959ebba-fbfc-4fc1–9705–64042206557f"}),
(a:Definition {uuid: '8caedfb2–4158–44a0-a617–3f8e1c34e2af'})
CREATE (p)-[r:DEFINES]->(a)
RETURN r;
MATCH (p:Publication {uuid:"8959ebba-fbfc-4fc1–9705–64042206557f"}),
(a:Definition {uuid: '5285a31c-f1d3–4bf6-b6d8–07d8e84c2360'})
CREATE (p)-[r:DEFINES]->(a)
RETURN r;
MATCH (p:Publication {uuid:"8959ebba-fbfc-4fc1–9705–64042206557f"}),
(a:Definition {uuid: '938d35cc-a8bd-4df9–8037–3fd199ede4d0'})
CREATE (p)-[r:DEFINES]->(a)
RETURN r;
MATCH (p:Publication {uuid:"8959ebba-fbfc-4fc1–9705–64042206557f"}),
(a:Definition {uuid: '5d2f4521–73c8–4660–89a3–3153d4abb271'})
CREATE (p)-[r:DEFINES]->(a)
RETURN r;
MATCH (p:Publication {uuid:"8959ebba-fbfc-4fc1–9705–64042206557f"}),
(a:Definition {uuid: '1c881ca3–61da-4c8a-8b6b-b3ee8e6c3323'})
CREATE (p)-[r:DEFINES]->(a)
RETURN r;
// Create relationships between definitions and elements
MATCH (a:Element {elementName: 'Actual Repurchases'}), (b:Definition
{uuid: '9be6d484–1187–4997–9a79–6784311e669b'})
CREATE (a)-[r:DEFINED_AS]->(b)
RETURN r;
MATCH (a:Element {elementName: 'Repurchase intentions'}), (b:Definition
{uuid: '534c33cd-9c2f-438b-b5f7-b5c1e89b1aa3'})
CREATE (a)-[r:DEFINED_AS]->(b)
RETURN r;
MATCH (a:Element {elementName: 'Swift guanxi'}), (b:Definition {uuid:
'9f62df02-e181–47e5–8108–6b4e2e9bcfbb'})
CREATE (a)-[r:DEFINED_AS]->(b)
RETURN r;
MATCH (a:Element {elementName: 'Trust'}), (b:Definition {uuid:
'02924d1f-7915–4aae-ab56–8b234d24af56'})
```

```
CREATE (a)-[r:DEFINED_AS]->(b)
RETURN r;
MATCH (a:Element {elementName: 'Presence'}), (b:Definition {uuid:
'8caedfb2–4158–44a0-a617–3f8e1c34e2af'})
CREATE (a)-[r:DEFINED_AS]->(b)
RETURN r;
MATCH (a:Element {elementName: 'Interactivity'}), (b:Definition {uuid:
'5285a31c-f1d3–4bf6-b6d8–07d8e84c2360'})
CREATE (a)-[r:DEFINED_AS]->(b)
RETURN r;
MATCH (a:Element {elementName: 'Effective use of instant messenger'}),
(b:Definition {uuid: '938d35cc-a8bd-4df9–8037–3fd199ede4d0'})
CREATE (a)-[r:DEFINED_AS]->(b)
RETURN r;
MATCH (a:Element {elementName: 'Effective use of message box'}),
(b:Definition {uuid: '5d2f4521–73c8–4660–89a3–3153d4abb271'})
CREATE (a)-[r:DEFINED_AS]->(b)
RETURN r;
MATCH (a:Element {elementName: 'Effective use of feedback system'}),
(b:Definition {uuid: '1c881ca3–61da-4c8a-8b6b-b3ee8e6c3323'})
CREATE (a)-[r:DEFINED_AS]->(b)
RETURN r;
// Create a graph for research model in the publication
CREATE (g:Model {ModelTitle: 'Research model', modelUUID:
'39b13ad8–6cce-492f-9998-b745ef9643f7'});
// Create the relationships between publication and the 'Research model'
MATCH (p:Publication {DOI: "10.25300/misq/2014/38.1.10"}),(g:Model
{uuid:"39aee9c5–2d5e-4ee1-b99a-a609175dba51"})
CREATE (p)-[r:CONTAINS]->(g)
RETURN r;
// Create relationships among elements
CREATE (:Relation {number: '1', uuid: 'e6e94576-cc36–493b-abfa-
dc99b4c43f02', type: 'Causal', relationDescription: ''});
MATCH (a:Element {elementName: 'Repurchase intentions'}), (c:Relation
{uuid: 'e6e94576-cc36–493b-abfa-dc99b4c43f02'})
CREATE (c)-[r:HAS{role: 'antecedent' }]->(a)RETURN r;
MATCH (b:Element {elementName: 'Actual Repurchases'}), (c:Relation
{uuid: 'e6e94576-cc36–493b-abfa-dc99b4c43f02'})
CREATE (c)-[r:HAS{role: 'consequent'}]->(b)RETURN r;
MATCH (m:Model {modelUUID: '39b13ad8–6cce-492f-9998-
b745ef9643f7'}), (c:Relation {number: '1',uuid: 'e6e94576-cc36–493b-abfa-
dc99b4c43f02', type: 'Causal'})
CREATE (m)-[r:DEPICTS]->(c)RETURN r;
CREATE (:Relation {number: '2', uuid: '72a8b0c2–09d3–45e5–8f88–
856fdb506d61', type: 'Causal', relationDescription: ''});
MATCH (a:Element {elementName: 'Swift guanxi'}), (c:Relation {uuid:
'72a8b0c2–09d3–45e5–8f88–856fdb506d61'})
```

CREATE (c)-[r:HAS{role: 'antecedent' }]->(a)RETURN r;
MATCH (b:Element {elementName: 'Repurchase intentions'}), (c:Relation {uuid: '72a8b0c2–09d3–45e5–8f88–856fdb506d61'})
CREATE (c)-[r:HAS{role: 'consequent'}]->(b)RETURN r;
MATCH (m:Model {modelUUID: '39b13ad8–6cce-492f-9998-b745ef9643f7'}), (c:Relation {number: '2',uuid: '72a8b0c2–09d3–45e5–8f88–856fdb506d61', type: 'Causal'})
CREATE (m)-[r:DEPICTS]->(c)RETURN r;
CREATE (:Relation {number: '3', uuid: 'c6e8351d-3eae-4eb7-b4d3–521e493516d8', type: 'Causal', relationDescription: ''});
MATCH (a:Element {elementName: 'Trust'}), (c:Relation {uuid: 'c6e8351d-3eae-4eb7-b4d3–521e493516d8'})
CREATE (c)-[r:HAS{role: 'antecedent' }]->(a)RETURN r;
MATCH (b:Element {elementName: 'Repurchase intentions'}), (c:Relation {uuid: 'c6e8351d-3eae-4eb7-b4d3–521e493516d8'})
CREATE (c)-[r:HAS{role: 'consequent'}]->(b)RETURN r;
MATCH (m:Model {modelUUID: '39b13ad8–6cce-492f-9998-b745ef9643f7'}), (c:Relation {number: '3',uuid: 'c6e8351d-3eae-4eb7-b4d3–521e493516d8', type: 'Causal'})
CREATE (m)-[r:DEPICTS]->(c)RETURN r;
CREATE (:Relation {number: '4', uuid: '022766c0–8ab4–422a-8a00–9ce577062baa', type: 'Causal', relationDescription: ''});
MATCH (a:Element {elementName: 'Trust'}), (c:Relation {uuid: '022766c0–8ab4–422a-8a00–9ce577062baa'})
CREATE (c)-[r:HAS{role: 'antecedent' }]->(a)RETURN r;
MATCH (b:Element {elementName: 'Swift guanxi'}), (c:Relation {uuid: '022766c0–8ab4–422a-8a00–9ce577062baa'})
CREATE (c)-[r:HAS{role: 'consequent'}]->(b)RETURN r;
MATCH (m:Model {modelUUID: '39b13ad8–6cce-492f-9998-b745ef9643f7'}), (c:Relation {number: '4',uuid: '022766c0–8ab4–422a-8a00–9ce577062baa', type: 'Causal'})
CREATE (m)-[r:DEPICTS]->(c)RETURN r;
CREATE (:Relation {number: '5', uuid: 'f1cf8eb0-b50b-420c-abc3-b7f8bdd19b8a', type: 'Causal', relationDescription: ''});
MATCH (a:Element {elementName: 'Interactivity'}), (c:Relation {uuid: 'f1cf8eb0-b50b-420c-abc3-b7f8bdd19b8a'})
CREATE (c)-[r:HAS{role: 'antecedent' }]->(a)RETURN r;
MATCH (b:Element {elementName: 'Trust'}), (c:Relation {uuid: 'f1cf8eb0-b50b-420c-abc3-b7f8bdd19b8a'})
CREATE (c)-[r:HAS{role: 'consequent'}]->(b)RETURN r;
MATCH (m:Model {modelUUID: '39b13ad8–6cce-492f-9998-b745ef9643f7'}), (c:Relation {number: '5',uuid: 'f1cf8eb0-b50b-420c-abc3-b7f8bdd19b8a', type: 'Causal'})
CREATE (m)-[r:DEPICTS]->(c)RETURN r;
CREATE (:Relation {number: '6', uuid: '1a62d0cf-9b50–4cc4-a239-d21f-981bf30d', type: 'Causal', relationDescription: ''});

MATCH (a:Element {elementName: 'Interactivity'}), (c:Relation {uuid: '1a62d0cf-9b50–4cc4-a239-d21f981bf30d'})
CREATE (c)-[r:HAS{role: 'antecedent' }]->(a)RETURN r;
MATCH (b:Element {elementName: 'Swift guanxi'}), (c:Relation {uuid: '1a62d0cf-9b50–4cc4-a239-d21f981bf30d'})
CREATE (c)-[r:HAS{role: 'consequent'}]->(b)RETURN r;
MATCH (m:Model {modelUUID: '39b13ad8–6cce-492f-9998-b745ef9643f7'}), (c:Relation {number: '6',uuid: '1a62d0cf-9b50–4cc4-a239-d21f981bf30d', type: 'Causal'})
CREATE (m)-[r:DEPICTS]->(c)RETURN r;
CREATE (:Relation {number: '7', uuid: '7031f457-ca92–446f-82e7-a7f1ed3ffcb7', type: 'Causal', relationDescription: ''});
MATCH (a:Element {elementName: 'Presence'}), (c:Relation {uuid: '7031f457-ca92–446f-82e7-a7f1ed3ffcb7'})
CREATE (c)-[r:HAS{role: 'antecedent' }]->(a)RETURN r;
MATCH (b:Element {elementName: 'Trust'}), (c:Relation {uuid: '7031f457-ca92–446f-82e7-a7f1ed3ffcb7'})
CREATE (c)-[r:HAS{role: 'consequent'}]->(b)RETURN r;
MATCH (m:Model {modelUUID: '39b13ad8–6cce-492f-9998-b745ef9643f7'}), (c:Relation {number: '7',uuid: '7031f457-ca92–446f-82e7-a7f1ed3ffcb7', type: 'Causal'})
CREATE (m)-[r:DEPICTS]->(c)RETURN r;
CREATE (:Relation {number: '8', uuid: '818cb865-e682–4fa0-b8b0-dd738a2e1f62', type: 'Causal', relationDescription: ''});
MATCH (a:Element {elementName: 'Presence'}), (c:Relation {uuid: '818cb865-e682–4fa0-b8b0-dd738a2e1f62'})
CREATE (c)-[r:HAS{role: 'antecedent' }]->(a)RETURN r;
MATCH (b:Element {elementName: 'Swift guanxi'}), (c:Relation {uuid: '818cb865-e682–4fa0-b8b0-dd738a2e1f62'})
CREATE (c)-[r:HAS{role: 'consequent'}]->(b)RETURN r;
MATCH (m:Model {modelUUID: '39b13ad8–6cce-492f-9998-b745ef9643f7'}), (c:Relation {number: '8',uuid: '818cb865-e682–4fa0-b8b0-dd738a2e1f62', type: 'Causal'})
CREATE (m)-[r:DEPICTS]->(c)RETURN r;
CREATE (:Relation {number: '9', uuid: '5cdb7900–0b1e-4fee-ad1c-886b3c14044e', type: 'Causal', relationDescription: ''});
MATCH (a:Element {elementName: 'Effective use of instant messenger'}), (c:Relation {uuid: '5cdb7900–0b1e-4fee-ad1c-886b3c14044e'})
CREATE (c)-[r:HAS{role: 'antecedent' }]->(a)RETURN r;
MATCH (b:Element {elementName: 'Interactivity'}), (c:Relation {uuid: '5cdb7900–0b1e-4fee-ad1c-886b3c14044e'})
CREATE (c)-[r:HAS{role: 'consequent'}]->(b)RETURN r;
MATCH (m:Model {modelUUID: '39b13ad8–6cce-492f-9998-b745ef9643f7'}), (c:Relation {number: '9',uuid: '5cdb7900–0b1e-4fee-ad1c-886b3c14044e', type: 'Causal'})
CREATE (m)-[r:DEPICTS]->(c)RETURN r;

```
CREATE (:Relation {number: '10', uuid: '25c41d47–89b3–4c03–8404–97371db32c7b', type: 'Causal', relationDescription: ''});
MATCH (a:Element {elementName: 'Effective use of instant messenger'}), (c:Relation {uuid: '25c41d47–89b3–4c03–8404–97371db32c7b'})
CREATE (c)-[r:HAS{role: 'antecedent' }]->(a)RETURN r;
MATCH (b:Element {elementName: 'Presence'}), (c:Relation {uuid: '25c41d47–89b3–4c03–8404–97371db32c7b'})
CREATE (c)-[r:HAS{role: 'consequent'}]->(b)RETURN r;
MATCH (m:Model {modelUUID: '39b13ad8–6cce-492f-9998-b745ef9643f7'}), (c:Relation {number: '10',uuid: '25c41d47–89b3–4c03–8404–97371db32c7b', type: 'Causal'})
CREATE (m)-[r:DEPICTS]->(c)RETURN r;
CREATE (:Relation {number: '11', uuid: '83ec6bfc-9fbd-469b-9b1c-dd0566bc15f7', type: 'Causal', relationDescription: ''});
MATCH (a:Element {elementName: 'Effective use of message box'}), (c:Relation {uuid: '83ec6bfc-9fbd-469b-9b1c-dd0566bc15f7'})
CREATE (c)-[r:HAS{role: 'antecedent' }]->(a)RETURN r;
MATCH (b:Element {elementName: 'Interactivity'}), (c:Relation {uuid: '83ec6bfc-9fbd-469b-9b1c-dd0566bc15f7'})
CREATE (c)-[r:HAS{role: 'consequent'}]->(b)RETURN r;
MATCH (m:Model {modelUUID: '39b13ad8–6cce-492f-9998-b745ef9643f7'}), (c:Relation {number: '11',uuid: '83ec6bfc-9fbd-469b-9b1c-dd0566bc15f7', type: 'Causal'})
CREATE (m)-[r:DEPICTS]->(c)RETURN r;
CREATE (:Relation {number: '12', uuid: '9391ae2a-1929–496c-bdde-9d7377e2a751', type: 'Causal', relationDescription: ''});
MATCH (a:Element {elementName: 'Effective use of message box'}), (c:Relation {uuid: '9391ae2a-1929–496c-bdde-9d7377e2a751'})
CREATE (c)-[r:HAS{role: 'antecedent' }]->(a)RETURN r;
MATCH (b:Element {elementName: 'Presence'}), (c:Relation {uuid: '9391ae2a-1929–496c-bdde-9d7377e2a751'})
CREATE (c)-[r:HAS{role: 'consequent'}]->(b)RETURN r;
MATCH (m:Model {modelUUID: '39b13ad8–6cce-492f-9998-b745ef9643f7'}), (c:Relation {number: '12',uuid: '9391ae2a-1929–496c-bdde-9d7377e2a751', type: 'Causal'})
CREATE (m)-[r:DEPICTS]->(c)RETURN r;
CREATE (:Relation {number: '13', uuid: '0606a583–4529–4719–9bda-ce5baa762d8b', type: 'Causal', relationDescription: ''});
MATCH (a:Element {elementName: 'Effective use of feedback system'}), (c:Relation {uuid: '0606a583–4529–4719–9bda-ce5baa762d8b'})
CREATE (c)-[r:HAS{role: 'antecedent' }]->(a)RETURN r;
MATCH (b:Element {elementName: 'Presence'}), (c:Relation {uuid: '0606a583–4529–4719–9bda-ce5baa762d8b'})
CREATE (c)-[r:HAS{role: 'consequent'}]->(b)RETURN r;
MATCH (m:Model {modelUUID: '39b13ad8–6cce-492f-9998-b745ef9643f7'}), (c:Relation {number: '13',uuid: '0606a583–4529–4719–9bda-ce5baa762d8b', type: 'Causal'})
```

```
CREATE (m)-[r:DEPICTS]->(c)RETURN r;
CREATE (:Relation {number: ‘14’, uuid: ‘1129d45d-ec7b-4b29-be90-f4fb-
10dd883e’, type: ‘Causal’, relationDescription: ‘’});
MATCH (a:Element {elementName: ‘Effective use of feedback system’}),
(c:Relation {uuid: ‘1129d45d-ec7b-4b29-be90-f4fb10dd883e’})
CREATE (c)-[r:HAS{role: ‘antecedent’ }]->(a)RETURN r;
MATCH (b:Element {elementName: ‘Interactivity’}), (c:Relation {uuid:
‘1129d45d-ec7b-4b29-be90-f4fb10dd883e’})
CREATE (c)-[r:HAS{role: ‘consequent’}]->(b)RETURN r;
MATCH (m:Model {modelUUID: ‘39b13ad8–6cce-492f-9998-
b745ef9643f7’}), (c:Relation {number: ‘14’,uuid: ‘1129d45d-ec7b-4b29-
be90-f4fb10dd883e’, type: ‘Causal’})
CREATE (m)-[r:DEPICTS]->(c)RETURN r;
// Create authors
CREATE (a:Author {ORCID: ‘0000–0001–8190–4009’,authorFirst: ‘Carol’,
authorLast: ‘Ou’, uuid:“c65809b0-e1ad-4829-a1ec-d03cf154fdf0”});
CREATE (a:Author {ORCID: ‘0000–0002–8830–5727’,authorFirst: ‘Paul’,
authorLast: ‘Pavlou’, uuid:“70bac363-e6f7–4556-abe0-d06c90bc1ba2”});
CREATE (a:Author {ORCID: ‘0000–0002–7243–3521’,authorFirst: ‘Robert’,
authorLast: ‘Davison’, uuid:“75d0a7b7–0e8e-4acd-bcbf-dadee1a7c1f6”});
// Create relationships between the authors and publication
MATCH (p:Publication {uuid:“8959ebba-fbfc-4fc1–9705–64042206557f”}),
(a:Author {uuid: ‘c65809b0-e1ad-4829-a1ec-d03cf154fdf0’})
CREATE (p)-[r:WRITTEN_BY {authorOrder: 1}]->(a)
RETURN r;
MATCH (p:Publication {uuid:“8959ebba-fbfc-4fc1–9705–64042206557f”}),
(a:Author {uuid: ‘70bac363-e6f7–4556-abe0-d06c90bc1ba2’})
CREATE (p)-[r:WRITTEN_BY {authorOrder: 2}]->(a)
RETURN r;
MATCH (p:Publication {uuid:“8959ebba-fbfc-4fc1–9705–64042206557f”}),
(a:Author {uuid: ‘75d0a7b7–0e8e-4acd-bcbf-dadee1a7c1f6’})
CREATE (p)-[r:WRITTEN_BY {authorOrder: 3}]->(a)
RETURN r;
// Create theories referenced in the publication
CREATE (:Theory {theoryTitle: ‘Media synchronicity theory’});
CREATE (:Theory {theoryTitle: ‘Social presence theory’});
MATCH (t:Theory {theoryTitle: ‘Media synchronicity theory’}),
(p:Publication {uuid:“8959ebba-fbfc-4fc1–9705–64042206557f”})
CREATE (p)-[r:DRAWS_ON]->(t)
RETURN r;
MATCH (t:Theory {theoryTitle: ‘Social presence theory’}), (p:Publication
{uuid:“8959ebba-fbfc-4fc1–9705–64042206557f”})
CREATE (p)-[r:DRAWS_ON]->(t)
RETURN r;
```

NOTE

1. Coding examples are based on Ou, C. X., Pavlou, P. A., & Davison, R. M. (2014). Swift Guanxi in online marketplaces: The role of computer-mediated communication technologies. *MIS Quarterly*, *38*(1), 209–230.

Appendix 2

FLOWCHART OF CODING PAPERS USING CODASAURUS

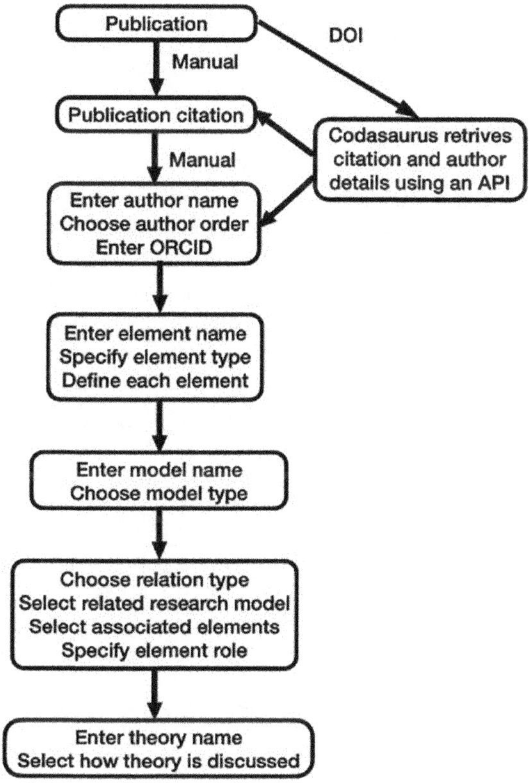

Source: Song et al., 2024

Figure A2.1 *Flowchart of coding a causal model*

Appendix 3

KEY CYPHER SYNTAX

The key Cypher syntax is summarized as follows. MATCH clause is used to specify what is looked for in the database, which can be either nodes or relationships. Based on the specificity of searching, the MATCH clause can be adapted accordingly using labels and properties. The examples in the table of the MATCH clause illustrate various searching purposes: searching for all nodes in the database, Theory nodes only, and the node representing agency theory. RETURN clause is used with the MATCH clause and specifies what needs to be retrieved from the match patterns, which can be a node, a relationship, or properties. WHERE clause is used to narrow a searching query stated in the MATCH clause. In the table, the MATCH clause searches for all elements, and the WHERE clause adds constraints that the elements of interest should contain "privacy" in the name. When one query cannot accomplish intended goals, the WITH clause is used to chain a set of query parts together. CREATE, DELETE, and SET can be used to modify the database by adding and deleting relationships or updating labels or properties of nodes and relationships. These clauses are building blocks of queries for efficient search of the knowledge network (Table A3.1).

Table A3.1 *Key Cypher queries*

Cypher keywords	Purpose	Examples
MATCH	The MATCH clause is used to search for patterns as described.	MATCH (t) MATCH (t:Theory) MATCH (t:Theory {theoryTitle:"Agency theory"})
RETURN	The RETURN clause is used to specify what should be retrieved.	MATCH p = (n:Publication)-[r]->(t:Theory {theoryTitle: "Agency theory"}) RETURN p
WHERE	The WHERE clause adds constraints to the patterns described in a MATCH clause	MATCH (n:Element) WHERE toLower(n.elementName) CONTAINS "privacy" RETURN n.elementName
WITH	The WITH clause links two query parts together, passing results from one to the next.	MATCH path = (l:Element)-[*]->(e:Element) Where toLower (e.elementName) Contains "performance" with path where not (:Element)-->(l) RETURN distinct [x IN NODES(path)|x. elementName] AS result
CREATE	The CREATE clause is used to create nodes and relationships.	CREATE (:Element {elementName: 'Shared knowledge', elementType: 'Construct' });
DELETE	The DELETE clause is used to delete nodes or relationships.	MATCH (e:Element {elementName: 'Shared knowledge'}) DETACH DELETE (n)
SET	The SET clause is used to update labels or properties of nodes and relationships.	MATCH (e:Element {elementName: 'Shared knowledge'}) SET e.elementType = 'Construct' return n

Appendix 4

PUBLICATION AND CURATION ID

The publications included in the 13 MISQ Curations discussed in this book are listed in Table A4.1, and the corresponding curation names for each ID are given in Table A4.2.The number of overlapped publications among the 13 MISQ Curations are shown in Table A4.3.

Table A4.1 Publications in the 13 MISQ Curations

Publication	**Curation ID**
Avgar, A., Tambe, P., & Hitt, L. M. (2018). Built to Learn: How Work Practices Affect Employee Learning During Healthcare Information Technology Implementation. *MIS Quarterly*, 42(2), 645–659.	1
Ayabakan, S., Bardhan, I., Zheng, Z. (Eric), … Kirksey, K. (2017). The Impact of Health Information Sharing on Duplicate Testing. *MIS Quarterly*, 41(4), 1083–1103.	1
Chan, J., & Ghose, A. (2012). Internet's Dirty Secret: Assessing the Impact of Online Intermediaries on the Outbreak of Sexually Transmitted Diseases (No. 12–07).	1
Kohli, R., Devaraj, S., & Ow, T. T. (2012). Does Information Technology Investment Influence a Firm's Market Value? A Case of Non-publicly Traded Healthcare Firms. *MIS Quarterly*, 1145–1163.	1
Menon, N. M. (2018). Information Spillover and Semi-Collaborative Networks in Insurer Fraud Detection. *MIS Quarterly*, 42(2), 407–426.	1
Sergeeva, A., Huysman,, M., Soekijad, M., … van den Hooff, B. (2017). Through the Eyes of Others: How Onlookers Shape the Use of Technology at Work. *MIS Quarterly*, 41(4), 1153–1178.	1

Publication	Curation ID
Salge, T. O., Kohli, R., & Barrett, M. (2015). Investing in Information Systems: On the Behavioral and Institutional Search Mechanisms Underpinning Hospitals' IS Investment Decisions. *MIS Quarterly*, 39(1), 61–90.	1
Srivastava, S. C., & Shainesh, G. (2015). Bridging the Service Divide Through Digitally Enabled Service Innovations: Evidence from Indian Healthcare Service Providers. *MIS Quarterly*, 39(1), 245–267.	1
Park, I., Sharman, R., & Rao, H. R. (2015). Disaster Experience and Hospital Information Systems: An Examination of Perceived Information Assurance, Risk, Resilience, and HIS Usefulness. *MIS Quarterly*, 39(2), 317–344.	1
Yeow, A., & Goh, K. H. (2015). Work Harder or Work Smarter?Information Technology and Resource Allocation in Healthcare Processes. *MIS Quarterly*, 39(4), 763–785.	1
Gao, G. (Gordon), Greenwood, B. N., Agarwal, R., … McCullough, J. S. (2015). Vocal Minority and Silent Majority: How Do Online Ratings Reflect Population Perceptions of Quality? *MIS Quarterly*, 39(3), 565–589.	1, 11
Kwon, J., & Johnson, M. E. (2014). Proactive Versus Reactive Security Investments in the Healthcare Sector. *MIS Quarterly*, 38(2), 451–471.	1, 12
Angst, C. M., Block, E. S., D'Arcy, J., … Kelley, K. (2017). When Do IT Security Investments Matter? Accounting for the Influence of Institutional Factors in the Context of Healthcare Data Breaches. *MIS Quarterly*, 41(3), 893–916.	1, 12
Paul, D. L., & McDaniel, R. R. (2004). A Field Study of the Effect of Interpersonal Trust on Virtual Collaborative Relationship Performance. *MIS Quarterly*, 28(2), 183.	1, 13
Angst, C. M., Wowak, K. D., Handley, S. M., … Kelley, K. (2017). Antecedents of Information Systems Sourcing Strategies in U.S. Hospitals: A Longitudinal Study. *MIS Quarterly*, 41(4), 1129–1152.	1, 5
Serrano, C., & Karahanna, E. (2016). The Compensatory Interaction Between User Capabilities and Technology Capabilities in Influencing Task Performance: An Empirical Assessment in Telemedicine Consultations. *MIS Quarterly*, 40(3), 597–621.	1, 6
Romanow, D., Rai, A., & Keil, M. (2018). CPOE-Enabled Coordination: Appropriation for Deep Structure Use and Impacts on Patient Outcomes. *MIS Quarterly*, 42(1), 189–212.	1, 6

Publication	Curation ID
Ray, G., Muhanna, W. A., & Barney, J. B. (2005). Information Technology and the Performance of the Customer Service Process: A Resource-Based Analysis. *MIS Quarterly*, 29(4), 625.	1, 6
Kohli, R., & Kettinger, W. J. (2004). Informating the Clan: Controlling Physicians' Costs and Outcomes. *MIS Quarterly*, 363–394.	1, 6
Lapointe, L., & Rivard, S. (2005). A Multilevel Model of Resistance to Information Technology Implementation. *MIS Quarterly*, 29(3), 461.	1, 6
Goh, J. M., Gao, G. (Gordon), & Agarwal, R. (2016). The Creation of Social Value: Can an Online Health Community Reduce Rural-Urban Health Disparities? *MIS Quarterly*, 40(1), 247–263.	1, 6
Ganju, K. K., Pavlou, P. A., & Banker, R. D. (2016). Does Information and Communication Technology Lead to the Well-Being of Nations? A Country-Level Empirical Investigation. *MIS Quarterly*, 40(2), 417–430.	1, 6
Mitchell, V. L. (2006). Knowledge Integration and Information Technology Project Performance. *MIS Quarterly,* 30(4), 919.	1, 7, 10
Dennis, A.R., & Garfield, M. J. (2003). The Adoption and Use of GSS in Project Teams: Toward More Participative Processes and Outcomes. *MIS Quarterly*, 27(2), 289.	1, 8
Angst, C. M., & Agarwal, R. (2009). Adoption of Electronic Health Records in the Presence of Privacy Concerns: The Elaboration Likelihood Model and Individual Persuasion. *MIS Quarterly*, 33(2), 339.	1,2
Kane, G. C., & Borgatti, S. (2011). Centrality-IS Proficiency Alignment and Workgroup Performance. *MIS Quarterly*, 35(4), 1063.	1,3
Venkatesh, V., Rai, A., Sykes, T. A., … Aljafari, R. (2016). Combating Infant Mortality in Rural India: Evidence from a Field Study of eHealth Kiosk Implementations. *MIS Quarterly*, 40(2), 353–380.	1,6
Lee, S.-Y., Rui, H., & Whinston, A. B. (2019). Is Best Answer Really the Best Answer? The Politeness Bias. *MIS Quarterly*, 43(2), 579–600.	10
Huang, P., Tafti, A., & Mithas, S. (2018). Platform Sponsor Investments and User Contributions in Knowledge Communities: The Role of Knowledge Seeding. *MIS Quarterly*, 42(1), 213–240.	10
Zhang, X. (2017). Knowledge Management System Use and Job Performance: A Multilevel Contingency Model. *MIS Quarterly*, 41(3), 811–840.	10

Publication	**Curation ID**
Majchrzak, A., Wagner, C., & Yates, D. (2013). The Impact of Shaping on Knowledge Reuse for Organizational Improvement with Wikis. *MIS Quarterly*, 37(2), 455–469.	10
Carlo, J. L., Lyytinen, K., & Rose, G. M. (2012). A Knowledge-Based Model of Radical Innovation in Small Software Firms. *MIS Quarterly*, 36(3), 865.	10
Beck, R., Pahlke, I., & Seebach, C. (2014). Knowledge Exchange and Symbolic Action in Social Media-Enabled Electronic Networks of Practice: A Multilevel Perspective on Knowledge Seekers and Contributors. *MIS Quarterly*, 38(4), 1245–1270.	10
Choi, S. Y., Lee, H., & Yoo, Y. (2010). The Impact of Information Technology and Transactive Memory Systems on Knowledge Sharing, Application, and Team Performance: A Field Study. *MIS Quarterly*, 34(4), 855.	10
Tanriverdi, H. (2005). Information Technology Relatedness, Knowledge Management Capability, and Performance of Multibusiness Firms. *MIS Quarterly*, 29(2), 311.	10
Poston, R. S., & Speier, C. (2005). Effective Use of Knowledge Management Systems: A Process Model of Content Ratings and Credibility Indicators. *MIS Quarterly*, 29(2), 221.	10
Ko, D.-G., Kirsch, L. J., & King, W. R. (2005). Antecedents of Knowledge Transfer from Consultants to Clients in Enterprise System Implementations. *MIS Quarterly*, 29(1), 59.	10
Bock, G.-W., Zmud, R. W., Kim, Y.-G., & Lee, J.-N. (2005). Behavioral Intention Formation in Knowledge Sharing: Examining the Roles of Extrinsic Motivators, Social-Psychological Forces, and Organizational Climate. *MIS Quarterly*, 29(1), 87.	10
Meyer, M. H., & Curley, K. F. (1991). An Applied Framework for Classifying the Complexity of Knowledge-Based Systems. *MIS Quarterly*, 15(4), 455.	10
Kankanhalli, A., Tan, B. C. Y., & Wei, K. K. (2005). Contributing Knowledge to Electronic Knowledge Repositories: An Empirical Investigation. *MIS Quarterly*, 29(1), 113.	10, 13
Nelson, K. M., & Cooprider, J. G. (1996). The Contribution of Shared Knowledge to IS Group Performance. *MIS Quarterly*, 20(4), 409. doi:10.2307/249562	10, 13
Wu, J., Huang, L., & Zhao, J. L. (2019). Operationalizing Regulatory Focus in the Digital Age: Evidence from an E-Commerce Context. *MIS Quarterly*, 43(3), 745–764.	11

Publication	Curation ID
Li, H., Fang, Y., Lim, K. H., … Wang, Y. (2019). Platform-Based Function Repertoire, Reputation, and Sales Performance of E-Marketplace Sellers. *MIS Quarterly*, 43(1), 207–236.	11
Huang, N., Hong, Y., & Burtch, G. (2017). Social Network Integration and User Content Generation: Evidence from Natural Experiments. *MIS Quarterly*, 41(4), 1035–1058.	11
Li, M., Tan, C.-H., Wei, K.-K., … Wang, K. (2017). Sequentiality of Product Review Information Provision: An Information Foraging Perspective. *MIS Quarterly*, 41(3), 867–892.	11
Jensen, M. L., & Yetgin, E. (2017). Prominence and Interpretation of Online Conflict of Interest Disclosures. *MIS Quarterly*, 41(2), 629–643.	11
Liu, Q. B., & Karahanna, E. (2017). The Dark Side of Reviews: The Swaying Effects of Online Product Reviews on Attribute Preference Construction. *MIS Quarterly*, 41(2), 427–448.	11
Luo, X., Gu, B., Zhang, J., … Phang, C. W. (2017). Expert Blogs and Consumer Perceptions of Competing Brands. *MIS Quarterly*, 41(2), 371–395.	11
Jabr, W., & Zheng, Z. (2014). Know Yourself and Know Your Enemy. *MIS Quarterly*, 38(3), 635–A10.	11
Yin, D., Bond, S. D., & Zhang, H. (2014). Anxious or Angry? Effects of Discrete Emotions on the Perceived Helpfulness of Online Reviews. *MIS Quarterly*, 38(2), 539–560.	11
Aggarwal, R., & Singh, H. (2013). Differential Influence of Blogs Across Different Stages of Decision Making: The Case of Venture Capitalists. *MIS Quarterly*, 37(4), 1093–1112.	11
Mudambi, S. M., & Schuff, D. (2010). Research Note: What Makes a Helpful Online Review? A Study of Customer Reviews on Amazon.com. *MIS Quarterly*, 34(1), 185.	11
Ba, S., & Pavlou, P. A. (2002). Evidence of the Effect of Trust Building Technology in Electronic Markets: Price Premiums and Buyer Behavior. *MIS Quarterly*, 26(3), 243. doi:10.2307/4132332	11, 13
Moody, G. D., Siponen, M., & Pahnila, S. (2018). Toward a Unified Model of Information Security Policy Compliance. *MIS Quarterly*, 42(1), 285–311.	12
Chen, Y., & Zahedi, F. M. (2016). Individuals' Internet Security Perceptions and Behaviors. *MIS Quarterly*, 40(1), 205–222.	12
Vance, A., Lowry, P. B., & Eggett, D. (2015). Increasing Accountability Through User-Interface Design Artifacts: A New Approach to Addressing the Problem of Access-Policy Violations. *MIS Quarterly*, 39(2), 345–366.	12

Publication	Curation ID
Boss, S. R., Galletta, D. F., Lowry, P. B., Moody, G. D., … Polak, P. (2015). What Do Systems Users Have to Fear? Using Fear Appeals to Engender Threats and Fear that Motivate Protective Security Behaviors. *MIS Quarterly*, 39(4), 837–864.	12
Johnston, A. C., Warkentin, M., & Siponen, M. (2015). An Enhanced Fear Appeal Rhetorical Framework: Leveraging Threats to the Human Asset Through Sanctioning Rhetoric. *MIS Quarterly*, 39(1), 113–134.	12
Wang, J., Gupta, M., & Rao, H. R. (2015). Insider Threats in a Financial Institution: Analysis of Attack-Proneness of Information Systems Applications. *MIS Quarterly*, 39(1), 91–112.	12
Willison, R., & Warkentin, M. (2013). Beyond Deterrence: An Expanded View of Employee Computer Abuse. *MIS Quarterly*, 37(1), 1–20.	12
Anderson, C. L., & Agarwal, R. (2010). Practicing Safe Computing: A Multimethod Empirical Examination of Home Computer User Security Behavioral Intentions. *MIS Quarterly*, 34(3), 613.	12
Gordon, L. A., Loeb, M. P., & Sohail, T. (2010). Market Value of Voluntary Disclosures Concerning Information Security. *MIS Quarterly*, 34(3), 567.	12
Johnston, A. C., & Warkentin, M. (2010). Fear Appeals and Information Security Behaviors: An Empirical Study. *MIS Quarterly*, 34(3), 549.	12
Bulgurcu, B., Cavusoglu, H., & Benbasat, I. (2010). Information Security Policy Compliance: An Empirical Study of Rationality-Based Beliefs and Information Security Awareness. *MIS Quarterly*, 34(3), 523.	12
Siponen, M., & Vance, A. (2010). Neutralization: New Insights into the Problem of Employee Information Systems Security Policy Violations. *MIS Quarterly*, 34(3), 487.	12
Harrington, S. J. (1996). The Effect of Codes of Ethics and Personal Denial of Responsibility on Computer Abuse Judgments and Intentions. *MIS Quarterly*, 20(3), 257.	12
Straub, D. W., & Nance, W. D. (1990). Discovering and Disciplining Computer Abuse in Organizations: A Field Study. *MIS Quarterly*, 14(1), 45.	12
Bapna, R., Qiu, L., & Rice, S. (2017). Repeated Interactions Versus Social Ties: Quantifying the Economic Value of Trust, Forgiveness, and Reputation Using a Field Experiment. *MIS Quarterly*, 41(3), 841–866.	13

Publication	Curation ID
Xiao, B., & Benbasat, I. (2011). Product-Related Deception in E-Commerce: A Theoretical Perspective. *MIS Quarterly*, 35(1), 169. doi:10.2307/23043494	13
Han, W., Ada, S., Sharman, R., … Rao, H. R. (2015). Campus Emergency Notification Systems: An Examination of Factors Affecting Compliance with Alerts. *MIS Quarterly*, 39(4), 909–929.	13
Burtch, G., Ghose, A., & Wattal, S. (2014). Cultural Differences and Geography as Determinants of Online Prosocial Lending. MIS Quarterly, 38(3), 773–794. doi:10.25300/misq/2014/38.3.07	13
Fang, Y., Qureshi, I., Sun, H., McCole, P., … Ramsey, E. (2014). Trust, Satisfaction, and Online Repurchase Intention: The Moderating Role of Perceived Effectiveness of E-Commerce Institutional Mechanisms. MIS Quarterly, 38(2), 407–427. doi:10.25300/misq/2014/38.2.04	13
Xiao, B., & Benbasat, I. (2007). E-Commerce Product Recommendation Agents: Use, Characteristics, and Impact. *MIS Quarterly*, 31(1), 137. doi:10.2307/25148784	13
Komiak, S. Y. X., & Benbasat, I. (2006). The Effects of Personalization and Familiarity on Trust and Adoption of Recommendation Agents. *MIS Quarterly*, 30(4), 941. doi:10.2307/25148760	13
Pavlou, P. A., & Fygenson, M. (2006). Understanding and Predicting Electronic Commerce Adoption: An Extension of the Theory of Planned Behavior. *MIS Quarterly*, 30(1), 115. doi:10.2307/25148720	13
Klein, R., & Rai, A. (2009). Interfirm Strategic Information Flows in Logistics Supply Chain Relationships. *MIS Quarterly*, 33(4), 735. doi:10.2307/20650325	13
Cyr, D., Head, M., Larios, H., & Pan, B. (2009). Exploring Human Images in Website Design: A Multi-Method Approach. *MIS Quarterly*, 33(3), 539. doi:10.2307/20650308	13
Sia, C.-L., Lim, K. H., Leung, K., Lee, M. K. O., Huang, W. W., & Benbasat, I. (2009). Web Strategies to Promote Internet Shopping: Is Cultural-Customization Needed? *MIS Quarterly*, 33(3), 491. doi:10.2307/20650306	13
Choudhury, V., & Karahanna, E. (2008). The Relative Advantage of Electronic Channels: A Multidimensional View. *MIS Quarterly*, 32(1), 179.	13
Gefen, D., Karahanna, E., & Straub, D. W. (2003). Trust and TAM in Online Shopping: An Integrated Model. *MIS Quarterly*, 27(1), 51. doi:10.2307/30036519	13

Publication	Curation ID
Wunderlich, P., Veit, D. J., & Sarker, S. (2019). Adoption of Sustainable Technologies: A Mixed-Methods Study of German Households. *MIS Quarterly*, 43(2), 673–691.	2
Adjerid, I., Peer, E., & Acquisti, A. (2018). Beyond the Privacy Paradox: Objective Versus Relative Risk in Privacy Decision Making. *MIS Quarterly*, 42(2), 465–488.	2
Gopal, R. D., Hidaji, H., Patterson, R. A., Rolland, E., … Zhdanov, D. (2018). How Much to Share with Third Parties?User Privacy Concerns and Website Dilemmas. *MIS Quarterly*, 42(1), 143–164.	2
Sutanto, J., Palme, E., Tan, C.-H., … Phang, C. W. (2013). Addressing the Personalization-Privacy Paradox: An Empirical Assessment from a Field Experiment on Smartphone Users. *MIS Quarterly*, 37(4), 1141–1164.	2
Hong, W., & Thong, J. Y. L. (2013). Internet Privacy Concerns: An Integrated Conceptualization and Four Empirical Studies. *MIS Quarterly*, 37(1), 275–298.	2
Smith, J., Dinev, T., & Xu, H. (2011). Information Privacy Research: An Interdisciplinary Review. *MIS Quarterly*, 35(4), 989.	2
Ayyagari, R., Grover, V., & Purvis, R. (2011). Technostress: Technological Antecedents and Implications. *MIS Quarterly*, 35(4), 831.	2
Son, J. Y., & Kim, S. S. (2008). Internet Users' Information Privacy-protective Responses: A Taxonomy and a Nomological Model. *MIS Quarterly*, 503–529.	2
Hui, K.-L., Teo, H. H., & Lee, S.-Y. T. (2007). The Value of Privacy Assurance: An Exploratory Field Experiment. *MIS Quarterly*, 31(1), 19.	2
Awad, N. F., & Krishnan, M. S. (2006). The Personalization Privacy Paradox: An Empirical Evaluation of Information Transparency and the Willingness to Be Profiled Online for Personalization. *MIS Quarterly*, 30(1), 13.	2
Culnan, M. J. (1993). "How Did They Get My Name?": An Exploratory Investigation of Consumer Attitudes toward Secondary Information Use. *MIS Quarterly*, 17(3), 341.	2
Pavlou, P. A., Liang, H. G., & Xue, Y. J. (2007). Understanding and Mitigating Uncertainty in Online Exchange Relationships: A Principal-Agent Perspective. *MIS Quarterly*, 31(1), 105.	2,13
Tavakolian, H. (1989). Linking the Information Technology Structure with Organizational Competitive Strategy: A Survey. *MIS Quarterly*, 13(3), 309. doi:10.2307/249006	3

Publication	Curation ID
Reich, B. H., & Benbasat, I. (2000). Factors That Influence the Social Dimension of Alignment between Business and Information Technology Objectives. *MIS Quarterly*, 24(1), 81. doi:10.2307/3250980	3
Soh, C., Markus, M. L., & Goh, K. H. (2006). Electronic Marketplaces and Price Transparency: Strategy, Information Technology, and Success. *MIS Quarterly*, 30(3), 705.	3
Banker, R. D., Hu, N., Pavlou, P.A., & Luftman, J. (2011). CIO Reporting Structure, Strategic Positioning, and Firm Performance. *MIS Quarterly*, 35(2), 487. doi:10.2307/23044053	3
Tallon, P. P., & Pinsonneault, A. (2011). Competing Perspectives on the Link Between Strategic Information Technology Alignment and Organizational Agility: Insights from a Mediation Model. *MIS Quarterly*, 35(2), 463. doi:10.2307/23044052	3
Xue, L., Ray, G., & Sambamurthy, V. (2012). Efficiency or Innovation: How Do Industry Environments Moderate the Effects of Firms' IT Asset Portfolios? *MIS Quarterly*, 36(2), 509. doi:10.2307/41703465	3
Gerow, J. E., Grover, V., Thatcher, J., … Roth, P. L. (2014). Looking Toward the Future of IT-Business Strategic Alignment through the Past: A Meta-Analysis. *MIS Quarterly*, 38(4), 1059–1085. doi:10.25300/misq/2014/38.4.10	3
Rai, A., Arikan, I., Pye, J., … Tiwana, A. (2015). Fit and Misfit of Plural Sourcing Strategies and IT-Enabled Process Integration Capabilities: Consequences of Firm Performance in the U.S. Electric Utility Industry. *MIS Quarterly*, 39(4), 865–885. doi:10.25300/misq/2015/39.4.6	3
Spears, J. l., & Barki, H. (2010). User Participation in Information Systems Security Risk Management. *MIS Quarterly*, 34(3), 503. doi:10.2307/25750689	3, 4, 12
Mani, D., Barua, A., & Whinston, A. (2010). An Empirical Analysis of the Impact of Information Capabilities Design on Business Process Outsourcing Performance. *MIS Quarterly*, 34(1), 39. doi:10.2307/20721414	3, 5
Wu, S. P.-J., Straub, D. W., & Liang, T.-P. (2015). How Information Technology Governance Mechanisms and Strategic Alignment Influence Organizational Performance: Insights from a Matched Survey of Business and IT Managers. *MIS Quarterly*, 39(2), 497–518. doi:10.25300/misq/2015/39.2.10	3,4
Majchrzak, A., Rice, R. E., Malhotra, A., King, N., & Ba, S. (2000). Technology Adaptation: The Case of a Computer-Supported Inter-Organizational Virtual Team. *MIS Quarterly*, 24(4), 569.	3,6,8

Publication	Curation ID
Pan, Y., Huang, P., & Gopal, A. (2016). Board independence and firm performance in the IT industry: The moderating role of new entry threats. *MIS Quarterly*, 42(3), 979–999.	4
Venkatesh, V., Sykes, T. A., Rai, A., & Setia, P. (2019). Governance and ICT4D Initiative Success: A Longitudinal Field Study of Ten Villages in Rural India. *MIS Quarterly*, 43(4).	4
Wang, E. T. G., Tai, J. C. F., & Grover, V. (2013). Examining the Relational Benefits of Improved Interfirm Information Processing Capability in Buyer-Supplier Dyads. *MIS Quarterly*, 37(1), 149–173.	4
Benitez, J., Ray, G., & Henseler, J. (2018). Impact of Information Technology Infrastructure Flexibility on Mergers and Acquisitions. *MIS Quarterly*, 42(1), 25–44.	4
Mindel, V., Mathiassen, L., & Rai, A. (2018). The sustainability of polycentric information commons. *MIS Quarterly*, 42(2), 607–632.	4
Susarla, A., & Mukhopadhyay, T. (2019). Can Outsourcing of Information Technology Foster Innovations in Client Organizations? An Empirical Analysis. *MIS Quarterly*, 43(3), 929–949. doi:10.25300/misq/2019/13535	4, 5
Goo, J., Kishore, R., Rao, H. R., & Nam, K. (2009). The Role of Service Level Agreements in Relational Management of Information Technology Outsourcing: An Empirical Study. *MIS Quarterly*, 33(1), 119. doi:10.2307/20650281	4, 5, 13
Dibbern, J., Winkler, J., & Heinzl, A. (2008). Explaining Variations in Client Extra Costs between Software Projects Offshored to India. *MIS Quarterly*, 32(2), 333. doi:10.2307/25148843	4, 5, 7
Gopal, A., & Koka, B. R. (2012). The Asymmetric Benefits of Relational Flexibility: Evidence from Software Development Outsourcing. *MIS Quarterly*, 36(2), 553. doi:10.2307/41703467	4, 5, 7
Rai, A., Maruping, L. M., & Venkatesh, V. (2009). Offshore Information Systems Project Success: The Role of Social Embeddedness and Cultural Characteristics. *MIS Quarterly*, 33(3), 617. doi:10.2307/20650313	4, 5, 7, 13
Tanriverdi, H. (2006). Performance Effects of Information Technology Synergies in Multibusiness Firms. *MIS Quarterly*, 30(1), 57.	4, 6
Jenkin, T. A., Chan, Y. E., & Sabherwal, R. (2019). Mutual Understanding in Information Systems Development: Changes Within and Across Projects. *MIS Quarterly*, 43(2), 649–671.	4, 7, 9

Publication	Curation ID
Moeini, M., & Rivard, S. (2019). Responding – or Not – to Information Technology Project Risks: An Integrative Model. *MIS Quarterly*, 43(2), 475–500.	4, 7, 9
Sengupta, K., & Te'eni, D. (1993). Cognitive Feedback in GDSS: Improving Control and Convergence. *MIS Quarterly*, 17(1), 87.	4, 8
Piccoli, G., & Ives, B. (2003). Trust and the Unintended Effects of Behavior Control in Virtual Teams. *MIS Quarterly*, 27(3), 365.	4, 8, 13
Miranda, S. M., & Kim, Y.-M. (2006). Professional Versus Political Contexts: Institutional Mitigation and the Transaction Cost Heuristic in Information Systems Outsourcing. *MIS Quarterly*, 30(3), 725. doi:10.2307/25148747	5
Han, K., & Mithas, S. (2013). Information Technology Outsourcing and Non-IT Operating Costs: An Empirical Investigation. *MIS Quarterly*, 37(1), 315–331. doi:10.25300/misq/2013/37.1.14	5
Hahn, E. D., Doh, J. P., & Bunyaratavej, K. (2009). The Evolution of Risk in Information Systems Offshoring: The Impact of Home Country Risk, Firm Learning, and Competitive Dynamics. *MIS Quarterly*, 33(3), 597.	5
Gefen, D., & Carmel, E. (2008). Is the World Really Flat? A Look at Offshoring at an Online Programming Marketplace. *MIS Quarterly*, 32(2), 367. doi:10.2307/25148844	5
Chang, Y. B., Gurbaxani, V., & Ravindran, K. (2017). Information Technology Outsourcing: Asset Transfer and the Role of Contract. *MIS Quarterly*, 41(3), 959–973. doi:10.25300/misq/2017/41.3.13	5
Chang, Y. B., & Gurbaxani, V. (2012). Information Technology Outsourcing, Knowledge Transfer, and Firm Productivity: An Empirical Analysis. *MIS Quarterly*, 36(4), 1043. doi:10.2307/41703497	5
Ang, S., & Straub, D. W. (1998). Production and Transaction Economies and IS Outsourcing: A Study of the U. S. Banking Industry. *MIS Quarterly*, 22(4), 535.	5
Susarla, A., Barua, A., & Whinston, A. B. (2003). Understanding the Service Component of Application Service Provision: An Empirical Analysis of Satisfaction with ASP Services. *MIS Quarterly*, 91–123.	5
Gefen, D., Wyss, S., & Lichtenstein, Y. (2008). Business Familiarity as Risk Mitigation in Software Development Outsourcing Contracts. *MIS Quarterly*, 32(3), 531. doi:10.2307/25148855	5, 7, 13

Publication	Curation ID
Ramasubbu, N., Mithas, S., Krishnan, M. S., & Kemerer, C. F. (2008). Work Dispersion, Process-Based Learning, and Offshore Software Development Performance. *MIS Quarterly*, 32(2), 437.	5, 7, 8
Vlaar, P. W. L., van Fenema, P. C., & Tiwari, V. (2008). Cocreating Understanding and Value in Distributed Work: How Members of Onsite and Offshore Vendor Teams Give, Make, Demand, and Break Sense. *MIS Quarterly*, 32(2), 227.	5, 8, 9
Ang, S., & Slaughter, S. A. (2001). Work Outcomes and Job Design for Contract versus Permanent Information Systems Professionals on Software Development Teams. *MIS Quarterly*, 25(3), 321.	5, 9
Ågerfalk, P. J., & Fitzgerald, B. (2008). Outsourcing to an Unknown Workforce: Exploring Opensurcing as a Global Sourcing Strategy. *MIS Quarterly*, 32(2), 385.	5, 9, 13
Benaroch, M., Lichtenstein, Y., & Fink, L. (2016). Contract Design Choices and the Balance of Ex Ante and Ex Post Transaction Costs in Software Development Outsourcing, *MIS Quarterly*, 40 (1), 57–82.	5,7
Subramani, M. R. (2004). How Do Suppliers Benefit from Information Technology Use in Supply Chain Relationships? *MIS Quarterly*, 28(1), 45.	6
Ahuja, M. K., & Thatcher, J. B. (2005). Moving beyond Intentions and toward the Theory of Trying: Effects of Work Environment and Gender on Post-Adoption Information Technology Use. *MIS Quarterly*, 29(3), 427. doi:10.2307/25148691	6
Sarker, S., & Valacich, J. S. (2010). An Alternative to Methodological Individualism: A Non-Reductionist Approach to Studying Technology Adoption by Groups. *MIS Quarterly*, 34(4), 779.	6
Zigurs, I., & Buckland, B. K. (1998). A Theory of Task/Technology Fit and Group Support Systems Effectiveness. *MIS Quarterly*, 22(3), 313.	6
Watson, R. T., DeSanctis, G., & Poole, M. S. (1988). Using a GDSS to Facilitate Group Consensus: Some Intended and Unintended Consequences. *MIS Quarterly*, 12(3), 463.	6
Compeau, D. R., & Higgins, C. A. (1995). Computer Self-Efficacy: Development of a Measure and Initial Test. *MIS Quarterly*, 19(2), 189. doi:10.2307/249688	6
Compeau, D., Higgins, C. A., & Huff, S. (1999). Social Cognitive Theory and Individual Reactions to Computing Technology: A Longitudinal Study. *MIS Quarterly*, 23(2), 145.	6

Publication	Curation ID
Christiaanse, E., & Venkatraman, N. (2002). Beyond Sabre: An Empirical Test of Expertise Exploitation in Electronic Channels. *MIS Quarterly*, 15–38.	6
Venkatesh, V., Thong, J. Y. L., & Xu, X. (2012). Consumer Acceptance and Use of Information Technology: Extending the Unified Theory of Acceptance and Use of Technology. *MIS Quarterly*, 36(1), 157.	6
Venkatesh, V., Morris, M. G., Davis, G. B., & Davis, F. D. (2003). User Acceptance of Information Technology: Toward a Unified View. *MIS Quarterly*, 27(3), 425.	6
Choudhury, V., Hartzel, K. S., & Konsynski, B. R. (1998). Uses and Consequences of Electronic Markets: An Empirical Investigation in the Aircraft Parts Industry. *MIS Quarterly*, 22(4).	6
Chatterjee, D., Grewal, R., & Sambamurthy, V. (2002). Shaping Up for E-Commerce: Institutional Enablers of the Organizational Assimilation of Web Technologies. *MIS Quarterly*, 26(2), 65.	6
Venkatesh, V., Brown, S. A., Maruping, L. M., & Bala, H. (2008). Predicting Different Conceptualizations of System Use: The Competing Roles of Behavioral Intention, Facilitating Conditions, and Behavioral Expectation. *MIS Quarterly*, 32(3), 483.	6
Turel, O., Serenko, A., & Giles, P. (2011). Integrating Technology Addiction and Use: An Empirical Investigation of Online Auction Users. *MIS Quarterly*, 35(4), 1043.	6
Boynton, A. C., Zmud, R. W., & Jacobs, G. C. (1994). The Influence of IT Management Practice on IT Use in Large Organizations. *MIS Quarterly*, 18(3), 299. doi:10.2307/249620	6
Tsai, H.-T., & Bagozzi, R. P. (2014). Contribution Behavior in Virtual Communities: Cogntiive, Emotional, and Social Influences. *MIS Quarterly*, 38(1), 143–163.	6
Bhattacherjee, A., & Premkumar, G. (2004). Understanding Changes in Belief and Attitude toward Information Technology Usage: A Theoretical Model and Longitudinal Test. *MIS Quarterly*, 28(2), 229. doi:10.2307/25148634	6
Goodhue, D. L., & Thompson, R. L. (1995). Task-Technology Fit and Individual Performance. *MIS Quarterly*, 19(2), 213. doi:10.2307/249689	6
Gray, P. H., Parise, S., & Iyer, B. (2011). Innovation Impacts of Using Social Bookmarking Systems. *MIS Quarterly*, 35(3), 629. doi:10.2307/23042800	6
Gefen, D., & Straub, D. W. (1997). Gender Differences in the Perception and Use of E-mail: An Extension to the Technology Acceptance Model. *MIS Quarterly*, 21(4), 389. doi:10.2307/249720	6

Publication	Curation ID
Gattiker, T. F., & Goodhue, D. L. (2005). What Happens after ERP Implementation: Understanding the Impact of Interdependence and Differentiation on Plant-Level Outcomes. *MIS Quarterly*, 29(3), 559. doi:10.2307/25148695	6
DeLone, W. H. (1988). Determinants of Success for Computer Usage in Small Business. *MIS Quarterly*, 12(1), 51.	6
Davis, F. D. (1989). Perceived Usefulness, Perceived Ease of Use, and User Acceptance of Information Technology. *MIS Quarterly*, 13(3), 319. doi:10.2307/249008	6
Liang, H., Saraf, N., Hu, Q., & Xue, Y. (2007). Assimilation of Enterprise Systems: The Effect of Institutional Pressures and the Mediating Role of Top Management. *MIS Quarterly*, 31(1), 59.	6
Karahanna, E., Xin Xu, S., Xu, Y., … Zhang, N. (2018). The Needs–Affordances–Features Perspective for the Use of Social Media. *MIS Quarterly*, 42(3), 737–756.	6
Karahanna, E., Agarwal, R., & Angst, C. M. (2006). Reconceptualizing Compatibility Beliefs in Technology Acceptance Research. *MIS Quarterly*, 30(4), 781.	6
Jung, J., Bapna, R., Ramaprasad, J., … Umyarov, A. (2019). Love Unshackled: Identifying the Effect of Mobile App Adoption in Online Dating. *MIS Quarterly*, 43(1), 47–72.	6
James, T. L., Wallace, L., & Deane, J. K. (2019). Using organismic integration theory to explore the associations between users' exercise motivations and fitness technology feature set use. *MIS Quarterly*, 43(1), 287–312.	6
Iacovou, C. L., Benbasat, I., & Dexter, A. S. (1995). Electronic Data Interchange and Small Organizations: Adoption and Impact of Technology. *MIS Quarterly*, 19(4), 465.	6
Rai, A., Pavlou, P., Im, G., & Du, S. (2012). Interfirm IT Capability Profiles and Communications for Cocreating Relational Value: Evidence from the Logistics Industry. *MIS Quarterly*, 36(1), 233.	6
Polites, G. L., & Karahanna, E. (2013). The Embeddedness of Information Systems Habits in Organizational and Individual Level Routines: Development and Disruption. *MIS Quarterly*, 37(1), 221–246.	6
Pinsonneault, A., & Rivard, S. (1998). Information Technology and the Nature of Managerial Work: From the Productivity Paradox to the Icarus Paradox? *MIS Quarterly*, 22(3), 287.	6

Publication	Curation ID
McElroy, J. C., Hendrickson, A. R., Townsend, A. M., & DeMarie, S. M. (2007). Dispositional Factors in Internet Use: Personality versus Cognitive Style. *MIS Quarterly*, 31(4), 809.	6
Maruping, L. M., & Magni, M. (2015). Motivating Employees to Explore Collaboration Technology in Team Contexts. *MIS Quarterly*, 39(1), 1–16.	6
Limayem, M., Hirt, S. G., & Cheung, C. M. K. (2007). How Habit Limits the Predictive Power of Intention: The Case of Information Systems Continuance. *MIS Quarterly*, 31(4), 705.	6
Seddon, P., Calvert, C., & Yang, S. (2010). A Multi-Project Model of Key Factors Affecting Organizational Benefits from Enterprise Systems. *MIS Quarterly*, 34(2), 305.	6
Schmitz, K. W., Teng, J. T. C., & Webb, K. J. (2016). Capturing the Complexity of Malleable IT Use: Adaptive Structuration Theory for Individuals. *MIS Quarterly*, 40(3), 663–686.	6
Tian, F., & Xu, S. X. (2015). How Do Enterprise Resource Planning Systems Affect Firm Risk? Post-Implementation Impact. *MIS Quarterly*, 39(1), 39–60.	6
Thompson, R. L., Higgins, C. A., & Howell, J. M. (1991). Personal Computing: Toward a Conceptual Model of Utilization. *MIS Quarterly*, 15(1), 125.	6
Thatcher, J. B., Wright, R. T., Sun, H., Zagenczyk, T. J., … Klein, R. (2018). Mindfulness in Information Technology Use: Definitions, Distinctions, and a New Measure. *MIS Quarterly*, 42(3), 831–847.	6
Beaudry, A., & Pinsonneault, A. (2010). The Other Side of Acceptance: Studying the Direct and Indirect Effects of Emotions on Information Technology Use. *MIS Quarterly*, 34(4), 689. doi:10.2307/25750701	6
Taylor, S., & Todd, P. (1995). Assessing IT Usage: The Role of Prior Experience. *MIS Quarterly*, 19(4), 561.	6
Sykes, T. A., Venkatesh, V., & Gosain, S. (2009). Model of Acceptance with Peer Support: A Social Network Perspective to Understand Employees' System Use. *MIS Quarterly*, 371–393.	6
Adams, D. A., Nelson, R. R., & Todd, P. A. (1992). Perceived Usefulness, Ease of Use, and Usage of Information Technology: A Replication. *MIS Quarterly*, 16(2), 227. doi:10.2307/249577	6
Banker, R. D., Bardhan, I. R., Chang, H., & Lin, S. (2006). Plant Information Systems, Manufacturing Capabilities, and Plant Performance. *MIS Quarterly*, 30(2), 315. doi:10.2307/25148733	6

Publication	Curation ID
Sun, H. (2012). Understanding User Revisions When Using Information System Features: Adaptive System Use and Triggers. *MIS Quarterly*, 36(2), 453.	6
Massey, A. P., & Montoya-Weiss, M. M. (2006). Unraveling the Temporal Fabric of Knowledge Conversion: A Model of Media Selection and Use. *MIS Quarterly*, 30(1), 99.	6, 10
Trantopoulos, K., von Krogh, G., Wallin, M. W., … Woerter, M. (2017). External Knowledge and Information Technology: Implications for Process Innovation Performance. *MIS Quarterly*, 41(1), 287–300.	6, 10
Arnold, V., Clark, N., Collier, P. A., Leech, S. A., & Sutton, S. G. (2006). The Differential Use and Effect of Knowledge-Based System Explanations in Novice and Expert Judgment Decisions. *MIS Quarterly*, 30(1), 79.	6, 10
Wasko, M. M., & Faraj, S. (2005). Why Should I Share? Examining Social Capital and Knowledge Contribution in Electronic Networks of Practice. *MIS Quarterly*, 29(1), 35.	6, 10
Wang, Y., Meister, D. B., & Gray, P. H. (2013). Social Influence and Knowledge Management Systems Use: Evidence from Panel Data. *MIS Quarterly*, 37(1), 299–313.	6, 10
Kim, S. H., Mukhopadhyay, T., & Kraut, R. E. (2016). When Does Repository KMS Use Lift Performance? The Role of Alternative Knowledge Sources and Task Environments. *MIS Quarterly*, 40(1), 133–156.	6, 10
Iyengar, K., Sweeney, J. R., & Montealegre, R. (2015). Information Technology Use as a Learning Mechanism: The Impact of IT Use on Knowledge Transfer Effectiveness, Absorptive Capacity, and Franchisee Performance. *MIS Quarterly*, 39(3), 615–641.	6, 10
Dennis, A. R., Fuller, R. M., & Valacich, J. S. (2008). Media, Tasks, and Communication Processes: A Theory of Media Synchronicity. *MIS Quarterly*, 32(3), 575. doi:10.2307/25148857	6, 8
Dennis, A. R. (1996). Information Exchange and Use in Group Decision Making: You Can Lead a Group of Information, but You Can't Make it Think. *MIS Quarterly*, 20(4) pp. 433–457.	6, 8
Bartelt, V. L., & Dennis, A. R. (2014). Nature and Nurture: The Impact of Automaticity and the Structuration of Communication on Virtual Team Behavior and Performance. *MIS Quarterly*, 38(2), 521–538.	6, 8

Publication	Curation ID
Huang, P., & Zhang, Z. (2016). Participation in Open Knowledge Communities and Job-Hopping: Evidence from Enterprise Software. *MIS Quarterly*, 40(3), 785–806. doi:10.25300/misq/2016/40.3.13	6, 9, 10
Ou, C. X., Pavlou, P. A., & Davison, R. M. (2014). Swift Guanxi in Online Marketplaces: The Role of Computer-Mediated Communication Technologies. *MIS Quarterly*, 38(1), 209–230.	6,13
Newman, M., & Sabherwal, R. (1996). Determinants of Commitment to Information Systems Development: A Longitudinal Investigation. *MIS Quarterly*, 20(1), 23.	7
Montealegre, R., & Keil, M. (2000). De-Escalating Information Technology Projects: Lessons from the Denver International Airport. *MIS Quarterly*, 24(3), 417.	7
Lee, G., & Xia, W. (2010). Toward Agile: An Integrated Analysis of Quantitative and Qualitative Field Data on Software Development Agility. *MIS Quarterly*, 34(1), 87.	7
Kudaravalli, S., Faraj, S., & Johnson, S. L. (2017). A Configural Approach to Coordinating Expertise in Software Development Teams. *MIS Quarterly*, 41(1), 43–64.	7
Keil, M., Tan, B. C. Y., Wei, K.-K., Saarinen, T., Tuunainen, V., & Wassenaar, A. (2000). A Cross-Cultural Study on Escalation of Commitment Behavior in Software Projects. *MIS Quarterly*, 24(2), 299.	7
Keil, M. (1995). Pulling the Plug: Software Project Management and the Problem of Project Escalation. *MIS Quarterly*, 19(4), 421.	7
Chen, Y., Bharadwaj, A., & Goh, K.-Y. (2017). An Empirical Analysis of Intellectual Property Rights Sharing in Software Development Outsourcing. *MIS Quarterly*, 41(1), 131–161.	7
Abdel-Hamid, T. K., Sengupta, K., & Swett, C. (1999). The Impact of Goals on Software Project Management: An Experimental Investigation. *MIS Quarterly*, 23(4), 531.	7
Iacovou, C. L., Thompson, R. L., & Smith, H. J. (2009). Selective Status Reporting in Information Systems Projects: A Dyadic-Level Investigation. *MIS Quarterly*, 33(4), 785. DOI:10.2307/20650327	7, 13
Barki, H., & Hartwick, J. (2001). Interpersonal Conflict and Its Management in Information System Development. *MIS Quarterly*, 25(2), 195.	7, 9
Stewart, K. J., & Gosain, S. (2006). The Impact of Ideology on Effectiveness in Open Source Software Development Teams. *MIS Quarterly*, 30(2), 291. DOI:10.2307/25148732	7, 9, 13

Publication	**Curation ID**
Zigurs, I., & Kozar, K. A. (1994). An Exploratory Study of Roles in Computer-Supported Groups. *MIS Quarterly*, 18(3), 277.	8
Srivastava, S. C., & Chandra, S. (2018). Social Presence in Virtual World Collaboration: An Uncertainty Reduction Perspective Using a Mixed Methods Approach. *MIS Quarterly*, 42(3), 779–803.	8
Saunders, C., Rutkowski, A. F., van Genuchten, M., Vogel, D., & Orrego, J. M. (2011). Virtual Space and Place: Theory and Test. *MIS Quarterly*, 35(4), 1079.	8
Majchrzak, A., Beath, C. B., Lim, R. A., & Chin, W. W. (2005). Managing Client Dialogues during Information Systems Design to Facilitate Client Learning. *MIS Quarterly*, 29(4), 653.	8
Alavi, M. (1994). Computer-Mediated Collaborative Learning: An Empirical Evaluation. *MIS Quarterly*, 18(2), 159.	8
Dennis, A. R., George, J. F., Jessup, L. M., Nunamaker, J. F., & Vogel, D. R. (1988). Information Technology to Support Electronic Meetings. *MIS Quarterly*, 12(4), 591.	8
Jessup, L. M., Connolly, T., & Galegher, J. (1990). The Effects of Anonymity on GDSS Group Process with an Idea-Generating Task. *MIS Quarterly*, 14(3), 313.	8
Gallupe, R. B., DeSanctis, G., & Dickson, G. W. (1988). Computer-Based Support for Group Problem-Finding: An Experimental Investigation. *MIS Quarterly*, 12(2), 277.	8
Dennis, A. R., Aronson, J. E., Heninger, W. G., & Walker, E. D. (1999). Structuring Time and Task in Electronic Brainstorming. *MIS Quarterly*, 23(1), 95.	8
Chidambaram, L., & Jones, B. (1993). Impact of Communication Medium and Computer Support on Group Perceptions and Performance: A Comparison of Face-to-Face and Dispersed Meetings. *MIS Quarterly*, 17(4), 465.	8
Curtis, A. M., Dennis, A. R., & McNamara, K. O. (2017). From Monologue to Dialogue: Performative Objects to Promote Collective Mindfulness in Computer-Mediated Team Discussions. *MIS Quarterly*, 41(2), 559–581.	8
Burke, K., & Chidambaram, L. (1999). How Much Bandwidth Is Enough? A Longitudinal Examination of Media Characteristics and Group Outcomes. *MIS Quarterly*, 23(4), 557.	8
Thomas, D. M., & Bostrom, R. P. (2010). Vital Signs for Virtual Teams: An Empirically Developed Trigger Model for Technology Adaptation Interventions. *MIS Quarterly*, 34(1), 115. doi:10.2307/20721417	8, 13

Publication	Curation ID
Kanawattanachai, P., & Yoo, Y. (2007). The Impact of Knowledge Coordination on Virtual Team Performance over Time. *MIS Quarterly*, 31(4), 783.	8,9,10,13
Zmud, R. W. (1983). The Effectiveness of External Information Channels in Facilitating Innovation within Software Development Groups. *MIS Quarterly*, 7(2), 43.	9
Watson, R. T. (1990). Influences on the IS manager's perceptions of key issues: Information scanning and the relationship with the CEO. *MIS Quarterly*, 217–231.	9
Venkatesh, V., Windeler, J. B., Bartol, K. M., … Williamson, I. O. (2017). Person–Organization and Person–Job Fit Perceptions of New IT Employees: Work Outcomes and Gender Differences. *MIS Quarterly*, 41(2), 525–558.	9
Rutner, P. S., Hardgrave, B. C., & McKnight, D. H. (2008). Emotional Dissonance and the Information Technology Professional. *MIS Quarterly*, 32(3), 635.	9
Reich, B. H., & Kaarst-Brown, M. L. (1999). "Seeding the Line": Understanding the Transition from IT to Non-IT Careers. *MIS Quarterly*, 23(3), 337.	9
Rasch, R. H., & Tosi, H. L. (1992). Factors Affecting Software Developers' Performance: An Integrated Approach. *MIS Quarterly*, 395–413.	9
Ransbotham, S., & Kane, G. C. (2011). Membership Turnover and Collaboration Success in Online Communities: Explaining Rises and Falls from Grace in Wikipedia. *MIS Quarterly*, 35(3), 613.	9
Moore, J. E. (2000). One Road to Turnover: An Examination of Work Exhaustion in Technology Professionals. *MIS Quarterly*, 24(1), 141.	9
Maruping, L. M., Daniel, S. L., & Cataldo, M. (2019). Developer Centrality and the Impact of Value Congruence and Incongruence on Commitment and Code Contribution Activity in Open Source Software Communities. *MIS Quarterly*, 43(3), 951–976.	9
Joseph, D., Ng, K. Y., Koh, C., & Ang, S. (2007). Turnover of Information Technology Professionals: A Narrative Review, Meta-Analytic Structural Equation Modeling, and Model Development. *MIS Quarterly*, 31(3), 547.	9
Jabr, W., Mookerjee, R., Tan, Y., … Mookerjee, V. S. (2014). Leveraging Philanthropic Behavior for Customer Support: The Case of User Support Forums. *MIS Quarterly*, 38(1), 187–208.	9

Publication	Curation ID
Igbaria, M., & Wormley, W. M. (1992). Organizational Experiences and Career Success of MIS Professionals and Managers: An Examination of Race Differences. *MIS Quarterly*, 16(4), 507.	9
Igbaria, M., Greenhaus, J. H., & Parasuraman, S. (1991). Career Orientations of MIS Employees: An Empirical Analysis. *MIS Quarterly*, 15(2), 151.	9
Igbaria, M., & Baroudi, J. J. (1995). The Impact of Job Performance Evaluations on Career Advancement Prospects: An Examination of Gender Differences in the IS Workplace. *MIS Quarterly*, 19(1), 107.	9
Goldstein, D. K., & Rockart, J. F. (1984). An Examination of Work-Related Correlates of Job Satisfaction in Programmer/ Analysts. *MIS Quarterly*, 8(2), 103.	9
Eesley, C., & Wu, L. (2020). For Startups, Adaptability and Mentor Network Diversity Can be Pivotal: Evidence from a Randomized Experiment on a MOOC Platform. *MIS Quarterly*, 44(2), 661–697.	9
Bassellier, G., & Benbasat, I. (2004). Business Competence of Information Technology Professionals: Conceptual Development and Influence on IT-Business Partnerships. *MIS Quarterly*, 28(4), 673.	9
Baroudi, J. J. (1985). The Impact of Role Variables on IS Personnel Work Attitudes and Intentions. *MIS Quarterly*, 9(4), 341.	9
Balijepally, V., Mahapatra, R., Nerur, S., & Price, K. H. (2009). Are Two Heads Better than One for Software Development? The Productivity Paradox of Pair Programming. *MIS Quarterly*, 33(1), 91.	9
Armstrong, D. J., & Hardgrave, B. (2007). Understanding Mindshift Learning: The Transition to Object-Oriented Development. *MIS Quarterly*, 31(3), 453.	9
Ahuja, M. K., Chudoba, K. M., Kacmar, C. J., McKnight, D. H., & George, J. F. (2007). IT Road Warriors: Balancing Work–Family Conflict, Job Autonomy, and Work Overload to Mitigate Turnover Intentions. *MIS Quarterly*, 31(1), 1.	9
Armstrong, D. J., Brooks, N. G., & Riemenschneider, C. K. (2015). Exhaustion from Information System Career Experience: Implications for Turn-Away Intention. *MIS Quarterly*, 39(3), 713–727.	9

Table A4.2 Correspondence between curation numbers and curation names

Number	Curation
1	Health Information Technology
2	Information Privacy
3	IS Alignment
4	IS Control and Governance
5	IS Sourcing
6	IS Use
7	IT Project Management
8	IT-supported Collaboration
9	IT Workforce
10	Knowledge Management
11	Online Word-of-Mouth
12	Securing Digital Assets
13	Trust

Table A4.3 The number of overlapped papers among the 13 curations

Curation ID	1	2	3	4	5	6	7	8	9	10	11	12	13
1	0	1	1	0	1	8	1	1	0	1	1	2	1
2	1	0	0	0	0	0	0	0	0	0	0	0	1
3	1	0	0	2	1	1	0	1	0	0	0	1	0
4	0	0	2	0	5	1	5	2	2	0	0	1	3
5	1	0	1	5	0	0	6	2	3	0	0	0	4
6	8	0	1	1	0	0	0	4	1	8	0	0	1
7	1	0	0	5	6	0	0	1	4	1	0	0	4
8	1	0	1	2	2	4	1	0	2	1	0	0	3
9	0	0	0	2	3	1	4	2	0	2	0	0	3
10	1	0	0	0	0	8	1	1	2	0	0	0	3
11	1	0	0	0	0	0	0	0	0	0	0	0	1
12	2	0	1	1	0	0	0	0	0	0	0	0	0
13	1	1	0	3	4	1	4	3	3	3	1	0	0

Appendix 5

SUPPLEMENTARY TABLES OF CONCEPT–TOPIC CORRESPONDENCE ANALYSIS

Correspondence analysis informs rows' (or columns') partial contributions to variance (Table A5.1 and Table A5.2). The reported eigenvalues indicate the amount of variance explained by a dimension. In this case, the first two dimensions account for 56.5 percent variance (Table A5.3), indicating that a two-dimensional transformation is appropriate for displaying the relationships among curations and concepts.

Examination of the curations indicates that dimension 1 is mainly explained by *Knowledge Management* (0.853) and *IS Use* (0.074); dimension 2 is mainly explained by *IT Workforce* (0.693) and *IS Use*

Table A5.1 Partial contributions of MISQ Curations

Curations	Dimension 1	Dimension 2
Health IT	0.003	0.009
Information Privacy	0.002	0.006
IS Alignment	0.000	0.004
IS Sourcing	0.003	0.008
IS Control and Governance	0.005	0.015
IS Use	0.074	0.151
IT Project Management	0.000	0.000
IT-supported Collaboration	0.003	0.000
IT Workforce	0.016	0.693
Knowledge Management	0.853	0.007
Online Word-of-Mouth	0.001	0.003
Securing Digital Assets	0.007	0.021
Trust	0.031	0.083

(0.151). Investigation of the concepts shows that dimension 1 is mainly explained by Quality of knowledge exchanged" (0.443) and "Knowledge transfer" (0.413); and dimension 2 is mainly explained by "Job satisfaction" (0.344) and "Work exhaustion" (0.25). The most frequent consequent concept in each curation is shown in Table A5.4.

Table A5.2 Partial contributions of concepts

Concepts	Dimension 1	Dimension 2
Trust	0.043	0.104
Usage	0.028	0.064
Performance	0.007	0.096
Job satisfaction	0.007	0.344
Perceived usefulness	0.021	0.053
Behavioral intention	0.017	0.048
Work exhaustion	0.005	0.250
Quality of knowledge exchanged	0.443	0.004
Computer-based information systems success	0.015	0.033
Knowledge transfer	0.413	0.004

Table A5.3 Variance explained by dimension

Dimension	Variance percentage	Cumulative variance percentage
1	29.98	29.98
2	26.53	56.51
3	24.92	81.43
4	10.04	91.47
5	5.19	96.66
6	3.34	100

Table A5.4 Most frequently studied consequent concept by curation

Curations	**1st concept**	**2nd concept**	**3rd concept**	**4th concept**	**5th concept**
Health Information Technology	Symbolic or substantive adoption	Infant mortality	Virtual collaborative relationship performance	Seeking professional medical care	E-consultation diagnosticity
Information Privacy	Intention to adopt smart metering technology	Privacy concern	Optimal publisher website price	Work overload	Strain
IS Alignment	IT investments	Strategy	Environmental turbulence	Social alignment	Financial performance
IS Sourcing	Satisfaction with application service providers	Job design characteristics	Perceived provider performance	Performance	Degree of IS outsourcing
IS Control and Governance	Modification flexibility	Buyer's manufacturing goals achievement	Project success	Supplier's relation-specific business process investments	Trust
IS Use	Usage	IT use	Perceived usefulness	Computer-based information systems success	Performance
IT Project Management	Selective reporting frequency	Project success	Extensiveness of coordination functions	Cognitive trust	Extensiveness of adaptability functions
IT-supported Collaboration	Task-knowledge coordination	Social presence	Team performance	Media synchronicity	Outcome

Curations	1st concept	2nd concept	3rd concept	4th concept	5th concept
IT Workforce	Turnover intention	Work exhaustion	Job satisfaction	Performance	Organizational commitment
Knowledge Management	Quality of knowledge exchanged	Knowledge transfer	Team performance	Current knowledge management systems use	Task-knowledge coordination
Online Word-of-Mouth	Sales performance	Credibility	Attribute importance	Prominence	Product referral centrality
Securing Digital Assets	Protection motivation	Intention	Perceived accountability	Attitude	Symbolic or substantive adoption
Trust	Trust	Attitude toward purchasing	Controllability of purchasing	Controllability of getting information	Task-knowledge coordination

References

Abu-Aisheh, Z., Raveaux, R., Ramel, J.-Y., & Martineau, P. (2015, January 10). *An exact graph edit distance algorithm for solving pattern recognition problems.* 4th International Conference on Pattern Recognition Applications and Methods 2015, Lisbon, Portugal.

Agrawal, R., Imieliński, T., & Swami, A. (1993). Mining association rules between sets of items in large databases. *Proceedings of the 1993 ACM SIGMOD International Conference on Management of Data, Washington DC, USA.*

Alavi, M., & Leidner, D. E. (2001). Knowledge management and knowledge management systems: conceptual foundations and research issues. *MIS Quarterly, 25*(1), 107–136.

Al Fawareh, H. M., Jusoh, S., & Osman, W. R. S. (2008, May 13–15). *Ambiguity in text mining.* 2008 International Conference on Computer and Communication Engineering, Kuala Lumpur, Malaysia.

Angrist, J. D., & Pischke, J.-S. (2009). *Mostly harmless econometrics: An empiricist's companion.* Princeton University Press.

Antons, D., Breidbach, C. F., Joshi, A. M., & Salge, T. O. (2021). Computational literature reviews: Method, algorithms, and roadmap. *Organizational Research Methods, 26*(1), 107–138. https://doi.org/10.1177/1094428121991230

Ba, S., & Pavlou, P. A. (2002). Evidence of the effect of trust building technology in electronic markets: Price premiums and buyer behavior. MIS quarterly, 243-268.

Barber, E. J. W., & Barber, P. (2005). *When they severed Earth from sky: How the human mind shapes myth.* Princeton University Press.

Bijmolt, T. H. A., Leeflang, P. S. H., Block, F., Eisenbeiss, M., Hardie, B. G. S., Lemmens, A., & Saffert, P. (2010). Analytics for customer engagement. *Journal of Service Research, 13*(3), 341–356. https://doi.org/10.1177/1094670510375603

Bloom, N., Jones, C. I., Van Reenen, J., & Webb, M. (2020). Are ideas getting harder to find? *American Economic Review, 110*(4), 1104–1144. https://doi.org/10.1257/aer.20180338

Boell, S., & Wang, B. (2019). www.litbaskets.io, an IT artifact supporting exploratory literature searches for information systems research. *Proceedings of the 2019 Australasian Conference on Information Systems, Perth, Australia.*

Boesl, F., Goereci, Y., Schweitzer, F., Finke, C., Schild, A.-K., Bittner, S., Steffen, F., Schröder, M., Quitschau, A., Heine, J., Warnke, C., & Franke, C. (2024). Cognitive decline in post-COVID-19 syndrome does not correspond with persisting neuronal or astrocytic damage. *Scientific Reports*, *14*(1). https://doi.org/10.1038/s41598-024-55881-1

Bolisani, E., Borgo, S., & Oltramari, A. (2012). Using knowledge as an object: challenges and implications. *Knowledge Management Research & Practice*, *10*(3), 202–205.

Bornmann, L., Haunschild, R., & Mutz, R. (2021). Growth rates of modern science: a latent piecewise growth curve approach to model publication numbers from established and new literature databases. *Humanities and Social Sciences Communications*, *8*(1). https://doi.org/10.1057/s41599-021-00903-w

Bosco, F. A. (2022). Accumulating knowledge in the organizational sciences. *Annual Review of Organizational Psychology and Organizational Behavior*, *9*, 441–464. https://doi.org/10.1146/annurev-orgpsych-012420–090657

Bosco, F. A., Field, J. G., Larsen, K. R., Chang, Y. Y., & Uggerslev, K. L. (2020). Advancing meta-analysis with knowledge-management platforms: Using metaBUS in psychology. *Advances in Methods and Practices in Psychological Science*, *3*(1), 124–137. https://doi.org/10.1177/2515245919882693

Budanitsky, A., & Hirst, G. (2006). Evaluating WordNet-based measures of lexical semantic relatedness. *Computational Linguistics*, *32*(1), 13–47. https://doi.org/10.1162/089120106776173093

Burt, R. S. (1992). *Structural holes*. Harvard University Press.

Caetano, T. S., McAuley, J. J., Cheng, L., Le, Q. V., & Smola, A. J. (2009). Learning graph matching. *IEEE Transactions on Pattern Analysis and Machine Intelligence*, *31*(6), 1048–1058.

Chen, Z., Li, X., & Bruna, J. (2017). Supervised community detection with line graph neural networks. arXiv preprint arXiv:1705.08415.

Chen, V. Z., Montano-Campos, F., & Zadrozny, W. (2020). Causal knowledge extraction from scholarly papers in social sciences. arXiv preprint arXiv:2006.08904.

Chen, V. Z., Montano-Campos, F., Zadrozny, W., & Canfield, E. (2021). Machine reading of hypotheses for organizational research reviews and pre-trained models via r shiny app for non-programmers. arXiv preprint arXiv:2106.16102.

Chomsky, N. (2002). On Nature and Language.

Conte, D., Foggia, P., Sansone, C., & Vento, M. (2004). Thirty years of graph matching in pattern recognition. *International Journal of Pattern Recognition and Artificial Intelligence*, *18*(3), 265–298. https://doi.org/10.1142/S0218001404003228

Corridoni, D., Antanaviciute, A., Gupta, T., Fawkner-Corbett, D., Aulicino, A., Jagielowicz, M., Parikh, K., Repapi, E., Taylor, S., Ishikawa, D., Hatano, R., Yamada, T., Xin, W., Slawinski, H., Bowden, R., Napolitani, G., Brain, O., Morimoto, C., Koohy, H., & Simmons, A. (2020). Single-cell atlas of colonic CD8+ T cells in ulcerative colitis. *Nature Medicine*, *26*(9), 1480–1490. https://doi.org/10.1038/s41591-020-1003-4

Cyr, D., Head, M., Larios, H., & Pan, B. (2009). Exploring human images in website design: a multi-method approach. MIS quarterly, 539-566.

Dann, D., Maedche, A., Teubner, T., Mueller, B., Meske, C., & Funk, B. (2019). DISKNET–A platform for the systematic accumulation of knowledge in IS research. *Proceedings of the 40th International Conference on Information Systems, Munich, Germany.*

Davis, M. F., Deveau, S., & Davalos, J. (2022, January 21). IBM sells some Watson Health assets for more than $1 billion. *Bloomberg.* www.bloomberg.com/news/articles/2022–01–21/ibm-is-said-to-near-sale-of-watson-health-to-francisco-partners

Denning, P. J. (2023). The smallness of large language models. *Communications of the ACM*, *66*(9), 24–27. https://doi.org/10.1145/3608966

Devlin, J., Chang, M.-W., Lee, K., & Toutanova, K. (2018). Bert: Pre-training of deep bidirectional transformers for language understanding. arXiv preprint arXiv:1810.04805.

Duan, Y., Cao, G., & Edwards, J. S. (2020). Understanding the impact of business analytics on innovation. *European Journal of Operational Research*, *281*(3), 673–686. https://doi.org/10.1016/j.ejor.2018.06.021

Duncan, O. D. (1966). Path analysis: Sociological examples [research article]. *American Journal of Sociology*, *72*(1), 1–16.

El Sawy, O. A., Malhotra, A., Park, Y., & Pavlou, P. A. (2010). Research commentary: Seeking the configurations of eigital ecodynamics: It takes three to tango [research article]. *Information Systems Research*, *21*(4), 835–848.

Francis, N., Green, A., Guagliardo, P., Libkin, L., Lindaaker, T., Marsault, V., Plantikow, S., Rydberg, M., Selmer, P., & Taylor, A. (2018). Cypher: An evolving query language for property graphs. *Sigmod'18: Proceedings of the 2018 International Conference on Management of Data*, 1433–1445. https://doi.org/10.1145/3183713.3190657

Freeman, L. C. (1977). A set of measures of centrality based on betweenness. *Sociometry*, 35–41.

Freeman, L. C. (1978). Centrality in social networks conceptual clarification. *Social Networks*, *1*(3), 215–239.

Gao, X. B., Xiao, B., Tao, D. C., & Li, X. L. (2010). A survey of graph edit distance. *Pattern Analysis and Applications*, *13*(1), 113–129. https://doi.org/10.1007/s10044-008-0141-y

Garfield, E. (1955). Citation indexes for science: A new dimension in documentation through association of ideas. *Science*(122), 108–111.

Geiger, D., Verma, T., & Pearl, J. (1990). *d*-Separation: From theorems to algorithms. In M. Henrion et al. (eds.), *Uncertainty in Artificial Intelligence: Machine Intelligence and Pattern Recognition Vol. 10* (pp. 139–148). Elsevier.

Goertz, G., & Press, P. U. (2006). *Social science concepts: A user's guide.* Princeton University Press.

Goldberger, A. S. (1972). Structural equation methods in the social sciences. *Econometrica*, *40*(6), 979–1001.

Gomaa, W. H., & Fahmy, A. A. (2013). A survey of text similarity approaches. *International Journal of Computer Applications*, *68*(13), 13–18.

Goo, J., Kishore, R., Rao, H. R., & Nam, K. (2009). The role of service level agreements in relational management of information technology outsourcing: An empirical study. MIS quarterly, 119-145.

Granger, C. W. J. (1969). Investigating causal relations by econometric models and cross-spectral methods. *Econometrica*, *37*(3), 424–438. https://doi.org/10.2307/1912791

Granovetter, M. S. (1973). The strength of weak ties. *American Journal of Sociology*, *78*(6), 1360–1380. https://doi.org/10.1086/225469

Greenacre, M. J. (1984). *Theory and applications of correspondence analysis*. Academic Press.

Grimshaw, J. (2010). *A Guide to Knowledge Synthesis*. Canadian Institues of Health Research. https://cihr-irsc.gc.ca/e/41382.html

Gurbaxani, V., & Dunkle, D. (2019). Gearing up for successful digital transformation. *Mis Quarterly Executive*, *18*(3), 209–220. https://doi.org/10.17705/2msqe.00017

Hagiu, A., & Wright, J. (2020). When data creates competitive advantage (and when it doesn't). *Harvard Business Review*, *98*(1), 94–101. <Go to ISI>://WOS:000504523800012

Halim, K. K., Halim, S., & Felecia. (2019). Business intelligence for designing restaurant marketing strategy: A case study. *Procedia Computer Science*, *161*, 615–622. https://doi.org/10.1016/j.procs.2019.11.164

Hentze, M. W., Castello, A., Schwarzl, T., & Preiss, T. (2018). A brave new world of RNA-binding proteins. *Nature Reviews Molecular Cell Biology*, *19*(5), 327–341. https://doi.org/10.1038/nrm.2017.130

Hernan, M. A., Hernandez-Diaz, S., & Robins, J. M. (2004). A structural approach to selection bias. *Epidemiology*, *15*(5), 615–625. https://doi.org/10.1097/01.ede.0000135174.63482.43

Herschel, R. T., Nemati, H., & Steiger, D. (2001). Tacit to explicit knowledge conversion: Knowledge exchange protocols. *Journal of Knowledge Management*, *5*(1), 107–116.

Hoffman, D. L., & Franke, G. R. (1986). Correspondence analysis: Graphical representation of categorical data in marketing research. *Journal of Marketing Research*, *23*(3), 213–227. https://doi.org/10.2307/3151480

Holland, P. W. (1986). Statistics and causal inference. *Journal of the American Statistical Association*, *81*(396), 945–960. https://doi.org/10.2307/2289064

Hume, D. (2003 [1739]). *A treatise of human nature*. Courier Corporation.

Hung, S.-H., Yao, C.-Y., Fang, Y.-J., Tan, P., Lee, R.-R., Sheffer, A., & Chu, H.-K. (2019). Micrography QR codes. *IEEE Transactions on Visualization and Computer Graphics*, *26*(9), 2834–2847.

Imai, K., Keele, L., Tingley, D., & Yamamoto, T. (2011). Unpacking the black box of causality: Learning about causal mechanisms from experimental and observational studies. *American Political Science Review*, *105*(4), 765–789.

Islam, A., & Inkpen, D. (2008). Semantic text similarity using corpus-based word similarity and string similarity. *ACM Transactions on Knowledge Discovery from Data (TKDD)*, *2*(2), 1–25.

Jaccard, P. (1912). The distribution of the flora in the Alpine zone. *New Phytologist*, *11*(2), 37–50.

Jones, B. F. (2009). The burden of knowledge and the "death of the Renaissance Man": Is innovation getting harder? *Review of Economic Studies*, *76*(1), 283–317. https://doi.org/10.1111/j.1467-937X.2008.00531.x

Jones, B. F. (2010). Age and great invention. *The Review of Economics and Statistics*, *92*(1), 1–14.

Karahanna, E., Benbasat, I., Bapna, R., & Rai, A. (2018). Opportunities and challenges for different types of online experiments. *MIS Quarterly*, *42*(4), iii–x.

Kelemen, D. (1999). The scope of teleological thinking in preschool children. *Cognition*, *70*(3), 241–272.

Kelemen, D. (2004). Are children "intuitive theists"? Reasoning about purpose and design in nature. *Psychological Science*, *15*(5), 295–301.

Kelley, T. L. (1927). *Interpretation of educational measurements*. World Book Co.

Krakovsky, M. (2022). Solving for why. *Communications of the ACM*, *65*(2), 11–13.

Kuhn, T. S. (1962). *The structure of scientific revolutions*. University of Chicago Press.

Lal, M. (2015). Neo4j graph data modeling. Packt Publishing Ltd.

Landauer, T. K., & Dumais, S. T. (1997). A solution to Plato's problem: The latent semantic analysis theory of acquisition, induction, and representation of knowledge. *Psychological Review*, *104*(2), 211–240.

Larsen, K. R., & Bong, C. H. (2016). A tool for addressing construct identity in literature reviews and meta-analyses. *MIS Quarterly*, *40*(3), 529–551. https://doi.org/10.25300/Misq/2016/40.3.01

Larsen, K. R., Hekler, E. B., Paul, M. J., & Gibson, B. S. (2020). Improving usability of social and behavioral sciences' evidence: A call to action for a national infrastructure project for mining our knowledge. *Communications of the Association for Information Systems*, 1–17. https://doi.org/10.17705/1cais.04601

Larsen, K. R., Hovorka, D. S., Dennis, A. R., & West, J. D. (2019). Understanding the elephant: The discourse approach to boundary identification and corpus construction for theory review articles. *Journal of the Association for Information Systems*, *20*(7), 887–927. https://doi.org/10.17705/1jais.00556

Lee, D. S., & Lemieux, T. (2010). Regression discontinuity designs in economics. *Journal of Economic Literature*, *48*(2), 281–355.

Lex, A., Gehlenborg, N., Strobelt, H., Vuillemot, R., & Pfister, H. (2014). UpSet: Visualization of intersecting sets. *IEEE Transactions on Visualization and Computer Graphics*, *20*(12), 1983–1992. https://doi.org/10.1109/tvcg.2014.2346248

Li, J. J., Larsen, K., & Abbasi, A. (2020). Theoryon: A design framework and system for unlocking behavioral knowledge through ontology learning. *MIS Quarterly*, *44*(4), 1733–1772.

Lim, S., Jatowt, A., Färber, M., & Yoshikawa, M. (2020). Annotating and analyzing biased sentences in news articles using crowdsourcing. *Proceedings of the Twelfth Language Resources and Evaluation Conference, Marseille, France.*

Liu, A., Wu, Z., Michael, J., Suhr, A., West, P., Koller, A., ... & Choi, Y. (2023). We're afraid language models aren't modeling ambiguity. arXiv preprint arXiv:2304.14399.

Lyu, J., Alberts, S., Rieke, G. H., & Rujopakarn, W. (2022). AGN selection and demographics in GOODS-S/HUDF from X-ray to radio. *The Astrophysical Journal, 941*(2). https://doi.org/10.3847/1538-4357/ac9e5d

Mahoney, J., Goertz, G., & Ragin, C. C. (2013). Causal models and counterfactuals. In S. L. Morgan (ed.), *Handbook of causal analysis for social research* (pp. 75–90). Springer.

Marois, R., & Ivanoff, J. (2005). Capacity limits of information processing in the brain. *Trends in Cognitive Sciences, 9*(6), 296–305. https://doi.org/10.1016/j.tics.2005.04.010

McKay, B. D., & Piperno, A. (2014). Practical graph isomorphism, II. *Journal of Symbolic Computation, 60*, 94–112. https://doi.org/10.1016/j.jsc.2013.09.003

Mihalcea, R., Corley, C., & Strapparava, C. (2006, July 16–20). *Corpus-based and knowledge-based measures of text semantic similarity.* National Conference on Artificial Intelligence, Boston, MA, USA.

Miller, G. A. (1995). WordNet: –A lexical database for English. *Communications of the ACM, 38*(11), 39–41. https://doi.org/10.1145/219717.219748

Misangyi, V. F., Greckhamer, T., Furnari, S., Fiss, P. C., Crilly, D., & Aguilera, R. (2017). Embracing causal complexity: The emergence of a neo-configurational perspective. *Journal of management, 43*(1), 255–282.

Mithas, S., Xue, L., Huang, N., & Burton-Jones, A. (2022). Causality meets diversity in information systems research. *MIS Quarterly, 46*(3), i–xvii.

Moody, G. D., Siponen, M., & Pahnila, S. (2018). Toward a unified model of information security policy compliance. *MIS Quarterly, 42*(1), 285–311. https://doi.org/10.25300/misq/2018/13853

Morgan, S. L. (2013). *Handbook of causal analysis for social research.* Springer.

Morgan, S. L., & Winship, C. (2015). *Counterfactuals and causal inference.* Cambridge University Press.

Mueller, R. M. (2015, January 5–8). *A meta-model for inferring inter-theory relationships of causal theories.* 48th Hawaii International Conference on System Sciences, Kauai, HI, USA.

Mueller, R. M., & Abdullaev, S. (2019, January 8–11). *DeepCause: Hypothesis extraction from information systems papers with deep learning for theory ontology learning.* 52nd Hawaii International Conference on System Sciences, Maui, HI, USA.

Mueller, R. M., & Huettemann, S. (2018). *Extracting causal claims from information systems papers with natural language processing for theory ontology learning.* 51st Hawaii International Conference on System Sciences, Waikola Village, HI, USA.

Nelson, L. K. (2019). To measure meaning in big data, don't give me a map, give me transparency and reproducibility. *Sociological Methodology, 49*(1), 139–143. https://doi.org/10.1177/0081175019863783

Nonaka, I., & von Krogh, G. (2009). Tacit knowledge and knowledge conversion: controversy and advancement in organizational knowledge creation theory. *Organization Science, 20*(3), 635–652. https://doi.org/10.1287/orsc.1080.0412

Nurse, P. (2021). Biology must generate ideas as well as data. *Nature, 597*(7876), 305. https://doi.org/10.1038/d41586–021–02480-z

Ou, C. X., Pavlou, P. A., & Davison, R. M. (2014). Swift Guanxi in online marketplaces: The role of computer-mediated communication technologies. *MIS Quarterly, 38*(1), 209–230.

Park, M., Leahey, E., & Funk, R. J. (2023). Papers and patents are becoming less disruptive over time. *Nature, 613*(7942), 138–144. https://doi.org/10.1038/s41586-022-05543-x

Pavlou, P. A., Liang, H., & Xue, Y. (2007). Understanding and mitigating uncertainty in online exchange relationships: A principal-agent perspective. MIS quarterly, 105-136.

Pearl, J. (1995). Causal diagrams for empirical research. *Biometrika, 82*(4), 669–688. https://doi.org/10.1093/biomet/82.4.669

Pearl, J. (2009). *Causality: Models, reasoning, and inference.* Cambridge University Press.

Pearl, J. (2017). Detecting latent heterogeneity. *Sociological Methods & Research, 46*(3), 370–389. https://doi.org/10.1177/0049124115600597

Pearl, J., & Mackenzie, D. (2018). *The book of why: the new science of cause and effect.* Basic Books.

Pearl, J., Glymour, M., & Jewell, N. P. (2016). *Causal inference in statistics: A primer.* John Wiley & Sons.

Piantadosi, S. T., Tily, H., & Gibson, E. (2012). The communicative function of ambiguity in language. Cognition, 122(3), 280-291.

Piccoli, G., & Ives, B. (2003). Trust and the unintended effects of behavior control in virtual teams. MIS quarterly, 365-395.

Polanyi, M. (1967). *The tacit dimension.* Routledge & Kegan Paul.

Ragin, C. C. (2014). *The comparative method: Moving beyond qualitative and quantitative strategies.* University of California Press.

Rai, A., & Bush, A. (2018). Editor's comments: MIS Quarterly Research Curations: Bundling for impact. *MIS Quarterly, 42*(3), iii–vi.

Sackett, D. L. (1979). Bias in analytic research. *Journal of Chronic Diseases, 32*(1–2), 51–63. https://doi.org/10.1016/0021-9681(79)90012-2

Shannon, C. E. (1948). A mathematical theory of communication. *Bell System Technical Journal, 27*(3), 379–423. https://doi.org/10.1002/j.1538-7305.1948.tb01338.x

Sokolov, A., Sabelli, F., Azadie faraz, B., Li, W., & Seco, L. A. (2024). Towards automating causal discovery in financial markets and beyond. *SSRN Electronic Journal.* https://doi.org/10.2139/ssrn.4679414

Song, Y., Watson, R., & Zhao, X. (2021). Literature reviewing: Addressing the jingle and jangle fallacies and jungle conundrum using graph theory and NLP. *Proceedings of the International conference on information systems 2021, Austin.*

Song, Y., Zhao, X., & Watson, R. T. (2024). Digitised knowledge-based literature reviewing: a tutorial on coding causal and process models as graphs. *Journal of Decision Systems*, 1–12. https://doi.org/10.1080/12460125.2023.2197705

Soni, J., & Goodman, R. (2017). *A mind at play: How Claude Shannon invented the information age.* Simon & Schuster.

Sowa, J. F. (1999). *Knowledge representation: Logical, philosophical and computational foundations.* Brooks/Cole Publishing Co.

Stokoe, C., Oakes, M. P., & Tait, J. (2003). Word sense disambiguation in information retrieval revisited. *Proceedings of the 26th Annual International ACM SIGIR Conference, New York, USA*.

Strickland, E. (2019). IBM Watson, heal thyself: How IBM overpromised and underdelivered on AI health care. *IEEE Spectrum*, *56*(4), 24–31.

Studer, R., Benjamins, V. R., & Fensel, D. (1998). Knowledge engineering: Principles and methods. *Data & Knowledge Engineering*, *25*(1–2), 161–197.

Sturm, B., & Sunyaev, A. (2019). Design principles for systematic search systems: A holistic synthesis of a rigorous multi-cycle design science research journey. *Business & Information Systems Engineering*, *61*(1), 91–111. https://doi.org/10.1007/s12599-018-0569-6

Suppes, P. (1973). A probabilistic theory of causality. *British Journal for the Philosophy of Science*, *24*(4).

Surowiecki, J. (2004). *The wisdom of crowds: Why the many are smarter than the few and how collective wisdom shapes business, economies, societies, and nations*. Doubleday.

Swanson, D. R. (1986). Undiscovered public knowledge. *The Library Quarterly*, *56*(2), 103–118.

Thilakaratne, M., Falkner, K., & Atapattu, T. (2019). A systematic review on literature-based discovery: General overview, methodology, & statistical analysis. *ACM Computing Surveys (CSUR)*, *52*(6), 1–34.

Thorndike, E. L. (1904). *An introduction to the theory of mental and social measurements*. Science Press.

Trkman, P., McCormack, K., de Oliveira, M. P. V., & Ladeira, M. B. (2010). The impact of business analytics on supply chain performance. *Decision Support Systems*, *49*(3), 318–327. https://doi.org/10.1016/j.dss.2010.03.007

Tukey, J. W. (1949). Comparing individual means in the analysis of variance. *Biometrics*, *5*(2). https://doi.org/10.2307/3001913

van de Schoot, R., de Bruin, J., Schram, R., Zahedi, P., de Boer, J., Weijdema, F., Kramer, B., Huijts, M., Hoogerwerf, M., & Ferdinands, G. (2021). An open source machine learning framework for efficient and transparent systematic reviews. *Nature Machine Intelligence*, *3*(2), 125–133.

Van de Ven, A. H. (2007). *Engaged scholarship: A guide for organizational and social research*. Oxford University Press.

Verweij, P. (2012). Twitter links between politicians and journalists. *Journalism Practice*, *6*(5–6), 680–691. https://doi.org/10.1080/17512786.2012.667272

Veuthey, A.-L., Pillet, V., Yip, Y. L., & Ruch, P. (2009). Text mining for Swiss-Prot curation: A story of success and failure. *Nature Precedings*. https://doi.org/10.1038/npre.2009.3166.1

Vial, G. (2019). Understanding digital transformation: A review and a research agenda. *The Journal of Strategic Information Systems*, *28*(2), 118–144.

Visser, L., Kalmar, J., Linkersdörfer, J., Görgen, R., Rothe, J., Hasselhorn, M., & Schulte-Körne, G. (2020). Comorbidities between specific learning disorders and psychopathology in elementary school children in Germany. *Frontiers in Psychiatry*, *11*. https://doi.org/10.3389/fpsyt.2020.00292

Wagner, G., Lukyanenko, R., & Paré, G. (2021). Artificial intelligence and the conduct of literature reviews. *Journal of Information Technology*, *37*(2), 209–226. https://doi.org/10.1177/02683962211048201

Wasserman, S., & Faust, K. (1994). Social network analysis: Methods and applications. Cambridge University Press.

Watson, R. T. (1996). *Data management: An organizational perspective*. Wiley.

Watson, R. T., & Webster, J. (2020). Analysing the past to prepare for the future: Writing a literature review a roadmap for release 2.0. *Journal of Decision Systems*, *29*(3), 129–147. https://doi.org/10.1080/12460125.2020.1798591

Watson, R. T., & Brancheau, J. C. (1991). Key issues in information-systems management: An international perspective. *Information & Management*, *20*(3), 213–223. https://doi.org/10.1016/0378-7206(91)90056-8

Watson, R. T., Kelly, G. G., Galliers, R. D., & Brancheau, J. C. (2015). key issues in information systems management: An international perspective. *Journal of Management Information Systems*, *13*(4), 91–115. https://doi.org/10.1080/07421222.1997.11518144

Watson, R. T., Plangger, K., Pitt, L., & Tiwana, A. (2022). A Theory of Information Compression: When Judgments Are Costly. *Information Systems Research*, *34*(3). https://doi.org/10.1287/isre.2022.1163

Watson, R. T., Song, Y., Zhao, X., & Webster, J. (2024). Extending the foresight of Phillip Ein-Dor: Causal knowledge analytics. *Journal of the Association for Information Systems*, *25*(1), 145–157. https://doi.org/10.17705/1jais.00871

Webster, J., & Watson, R. T. (2002). Analyzing the past to prepare for the future: Writing a literature review. *MIS Quarterly*, *26*(2), xiii–xxiii.

Willett, P. (2006). The Porter stemming algorithm: Then and now. *Program-Electronic Library and Information Systems*, *40*(3), 219–223. https://doi.org/10.1108/00330330610681295

Winding, M., Pedigo, B. D., Barnes, C. L., Patsolic, H. G., Park, Y., Kazimiers, T., Fushiki, A., Andrade, I. V., Khandelwal, A., Valdes-Aleman, J., Li, F., Randel, N., Barsotti, E., Correia, A., Fetter, R. D., Hartenstein, V., Priebe, C. E., Vogelstein, J. T., Cardona, A., & Zlatic, M. (2023). The connectome of an insect brain. *Science*, *379*(6636). https://doi.org/10.1126/science.add9330

Wixom, B. H., Yen, B., & Relich, M. (2013). Maximizing Value from Business Analytics. *Mis Quarterly Executive*, *12*(2), 111–123. <Go to ISI>://WOS:000320010800005

Woodward, J. (2005). *Making things happen: A theory of causal explanation*. Oxford University Press.

Xiao, B., & Benbasat, I. (2007). E-commerce product recommendation agents: Use, characteristics, and impact. MIS quarterly, 137-209.

Yan, J., Yin, X.-C., Lin, W., Deng, C., Zha, H., & Yang, X. (2016). A short survey of recent advances in graph matching. *Proceedings of the 2016 ACM on International Conference on Multimedia Retrieval*, New York, USA.

Yelland, P. M. (2010). An introduction to correspondence analysis. *The Mathematica Journal*, *12*(1), 86–109.

Zeng, Z., Tung, A. K., Wang, J., Feng, J., & Zhou, L. (2009). Comparing stars: On approximating graph edit distance. *Proceedings of the VLDB Endowment*, *2*(1), 25–36.
Zhang, M., & Chen, Y. (2018). Link prediction based on graph neural networks. Advances in neural information processing systems, 31.
Zupko, R. E. (1990). Revolution in measurement: Western European weights and measures since the age of science(Vol. 186). American Philosophical Society.

Index